THE VICTORIA HISTORY OF MIDDLESEX

KNIGHTSBRIDGE AND HYDE

Pamela Taylor

First published 2017

A Victoria County History publication

© The University of London, 2017

ISBN 978-1-909646-66-7

Cover image: Trinity chapel after its 1789 refronting (H.G. Davis, *Memorials of the Hamlet of Knightsbridge*, 1859).
Back cover image: The Royal Albert Hall (Shutterstock/Dan Breckwoldt).

Typeset in Minion Pro by Jessica Davies

CONTENTS

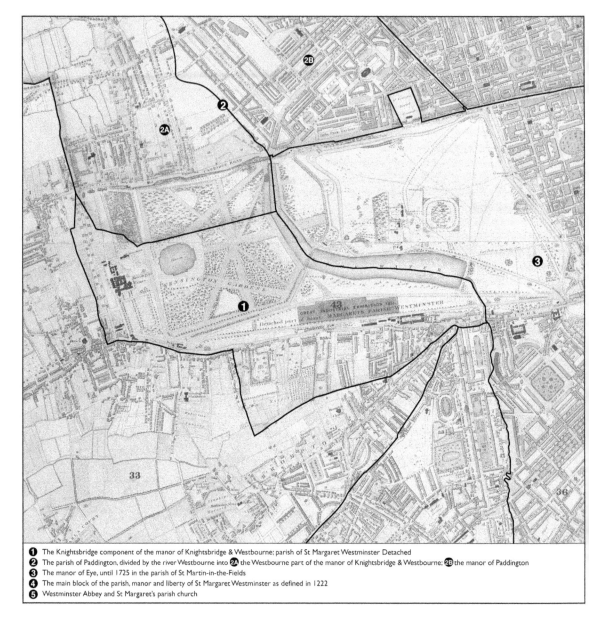

1. The Knightsbridge component of the manor of Knightsbridge & Westbourne; parish of St Margaret Westminster Detached
2. The parish of Paddington, divided by the river Westbourne into 2A the Westbourne part of the manor of Knightsbridge & Westbourne; 2B the manor of Paddington
3. The manor of Eye, until 1725 in the parish of St Martin-in-the-Fields
4. The main block of the parish, manor and liberty of St Margaret Westminster as defined in 1222
5. Westminster Abbey and St Margaret's parish church

Frontispiece *The manor of Knightsbridge. Extract from Greenwood's Map of London, 1854, highlighted to show the key manor and parish boundaries.*

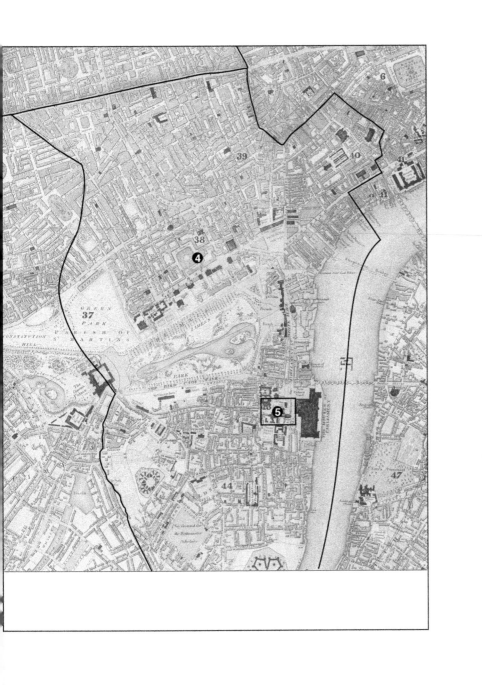

LIST OF ILLUSTRATIONS

All photographs taken by Pamela Taylor in 2016 unless otherwise stated.

Figure

Map

FOREWORD

From its foundation Westminster Abbey was one of the largest of the church landholders. Royal grants of land from the 10th to the 16th century, reflections of royal favour, form some of the most important documents in the abbey's muniment room. The loss of all of the abbey estates in 1868, when they were amalgamated with those of other cathedrals into the holdings of the Ecclesiastical Commissioners (in return for an annual sum of £20,000), changed the emphasis of the dean and chapter's work beyond recognition.

The history of these estates has been told in many forms, from Barbara Harvey's broad analysis, to individual studies of particular localities. But there are of course a great many gaps in our knowledge. The addition of Pamela Taylor's masterful work on the manors of Knightsbridge and Hyde, an area of London apparently so well known, but whose history has evidently been misunderstood for so long, is greatly to be welcomed. Her painstaking scholarship in unpicking the precise boundaries of these and surrounding areas, and the alterations made to them in the last thousand years, is of profound and lasting value. I am delighted that this work was made possible very largely through the use of the abbey's own archives.

It is well known that the *Victoria County History* is a work of such fundamental importance to the history of this country, that all scholars, all historians, both national and local, indeed all interested parties, are forever in its debt. The new series of *VCH* 'shorts', of which this volume forms the first 'Victoria History of Middlesex' edition, is a laudable extension to this series.

It is therefore with great pleasure that I commend this important work of scholarship, which I have personally found both hugely interesting and enlightening, and which will clearly form the basis of all subsequent studies of the area.

The Very Reverend Dr John Hall
Dean of Westminster

ACKNOWLEDGEMENTS

THIS BOOK COULD NOT have been written without the generous support and encouragement of Patricia Croot and Alan Thacker, respectively main author and editor of *VCH Middlesex*, XIII, and of Adam Chapman, Matthew Bristow, Jessica Davies and her successor, Lianne Sherlock, of the Victoria County History's Central Office. I also owe a special debt to Olivia Fryman, editor of *Kensington Palace* (forthcoming), for discussion and source-sharing. Thanks too to Barbara Harvey, Derek Keene, Julia Merritt, Susan Reynolds, Tim Tatton-Brown and Andrew Wareham for discussion and advice. It is also a pleasure to thank the many archivists and librarians whose help has made the research so enjoyable, especially Matthew Payne, Tony Trowles and Christine Reynolds at Westminster Abbey; Alison Kenney and her colleagues at WCA together with Louise Martin at Grosvenor Eaton; the staff at KLS; cartographer Cath D'Alton; Olwen Myhill of the Institute of Historical Research's Centre for Metropolitan History; and Penny Hatfield at Eton College. Funding was granted by the Victoria County History Trust to support the cartography and printing of the book.

KNIGHTSBRIDGE WAS NOT AN ancient parish, which makes it an unusual subject for a VCH account, and both the area and this book's coverage of it are also unusual. Today's Knightsbridge is famously the wealthy shoppers' paradise centred on the Brompton Road and Harrods, but until the later 19th century Knightsbridge was centred on the part of the main road between London and the west named, in 2016, Knightsbridge, Kensington Road and Kensington Gore. Henry Davis, whose *Memorials of the Hamlet of Knightsbridge* (1859) is still essential and enjoyable reading, paid little attention to the Brompton Road not only because it was almost entirely in Kensington – as its southern side, including Harrods, still is – but because it was not yet important. High streets are almost always a straightforward update of a village or hamlet's main road so the shift hints at deeper issues.

This book has two main purposes: to uncover early Knightsbridge, which was a major and well-documented Westminster Abbey manor within – it turns out – easily recoverable borders, and, just as importantly, to understand why the memory of its true

Figure 1 *Knightsbridge looking west past its closely adjacent junctions with Sloane Street and Brompton Road.*

extent and early history has been so comprehensively lost. This occlusion or loss is the
result of a unique series of misfortunes, each of them of more than local interest, which
together ensured that much of what was actually Knightsbridge came to be thought of
only in terms of Westminster, Hyde or Kensington.

Among these misfortunes were Knightsbridge's failure to become a separate parish
and its particularly complicated relationship with the mother parish of St Margaret
Westminster. The mid 14th-century decision to manage some of the demesne lands in
a single unit with those of neighbouring Hyde – the latter until then entirely part of the
adjacent manor of Eye – meant that soon after Henry VIII removed all of Eye from the
abbey a large part of Knightsbridge quietly vanished along with Hyde into the new Hyde
Park. A separate, equally unhelpful development was the 1689 sale of an estate west of
Hyde Park to William III. This was part of Knightsbridge but it became Kensington
Palace and all the consequent royal kudos flowed to Kensington, so much so that in
1900 the local government boundaries were shifted to put the palace into Kensington.
The royal link also helps explain why the museums area, the 87-a. estate purchased and
developed by the 1851 Commissioners in furtherance of Prince Albert's plan to use the
profits of the Great Exhibition to extend the influence of science and art upon productive
industry, was named South Kensington. The cumulative result of all this was that the
name of Knightsbridge lost its hold on the actual, wider area and came to mean only the
(in fact) cross-border settlement at its south-eastern corner.

Confusion about Knightsbridge's extent has bedevilled all previous studies, and a
brief survey will highlight some of the problems. Davis was very unusual in realising that
Knightsbridge was fundamentally in the parish of St Margaret Westminster, even though
by his time the hamlet settlement had expanded into three adjacent ancient parishes:
St Martin-in-the-Fields (since 1725, St George Hanover Square), St Mary Abbotts
Kensington and St Luke Chelsea. He also made his own extensions by including parts of
Belgravia and Pimlico because they had been assigned to St Paul's Knightsbridge (1840)
but correctly drew no deeper connection. He also realised that Knightsbridge covered
more than its built-up hamlet and that Westminster Abbey had lands there before
1066, but he had no access to the abbey muniments, missed a helpful article published
in 1836, and was unable to make the crucial manor-parish link.[1] Hence his statement
that: 'The whole of this isolated [i.e., detached] part of St Margaret's, including a part of
Kensington, its palace and gardens, are included in the manor of Knightsbridge'.[2] And
even Davis, unable to establish in which parish Eye, which included Hyde, had originally
lain, fell back on the casual argument of unassigned forest and marsh.[3]

Davis's followers were embarrassingly happy to copy him on Knightsbridge hamlet
and its distinguished inhabitants but ignored his statements on the underlying structure,
with such unfortunate results as this from Edward Walford (1878): 'In the early Saxon
days, when "Chelsey," and "Kensing town," and "Charing" were country villages, there lay
between all three a sort of "No Man's Land," which in process of time came to be called
"Knightsbridge," although it never assumed, or even claimed, parochial honours, nor
indeed could it be said to have had a recognised existence. It was a district of uncertain

---

1   Saunders, 'Extent of Westminster'.
2   Davis, *Knightsbridge*, 7.
3   Ibid., 48.

extent and limits; but it is, nevertheless, our purpose to try and "beat the bounds" on behalf of its former inhabitants. The name of Knightsbridge, then, must be taken as indicating, not a parish, nor yet a manor, but only a certain locality adjoining a bridge, which formerly stood on the road between London and far distant Kensington.'[4]

This nonsense is perpetuated in the otherwise excellent *Survey of London* (2000) which ignores the manorial framework and therefore claims that Knightsbridge's 'southern extent is indeterminate and always has been', while the most recent edition of Pevsner's *Westminster* (2003) places all of it under Belgravia.[5] The official history of Kensington Palace published in 2003 notably failed to realise that until 1900 Kensington Palace was not in Kensington.[6] Instead it claimed that Kensington had stretched as far east as Eye/Hyde in Domesday Book (1086) and had been reassembled by Sir Walter Cope *c.*1600. It also claimed with equal inaccuracy that both of Eye's boundary rivers, the Tyburn as well as the Westbourne, ran across Hyde Park.[7]

Even for historians who know the importance of the manor and parish framework there have been problems. Knightsbridge manor always also included Westbourne, adjacent on the north, and was known both as Knightsbridge and, by 1511, Knightsbridge & Westbourne manor. The river Westbourne provided the manor's eastern boundary but there were two eastward links that have sown confusion. In 1222 St Margaret Detached still contained three vills: Knightsbridge, Westbourne and, immediately east of Westbourne, Paddington, but Paddington later became a parish which, by 1452, also covered Westbourne.[8] The linkage of the three cuts across parish-based frameworks and has therefore been overlooked. Saunders came closest to understanding the interconnection but regarded all three as separate manors.[9] Neither *VCH Middlesex*, IX which includes Paddington parish nor *VCH Middlesex*, XIII, thus far the only volume of an intended four for Westminster, registers that Westbourne, Paddington and Knightsbridge were initially all within Westminster, and Westbourne is given entirely to *VCH Middlesex*, IX even though it remained part of Knightsbridge manor. The Knightsbridge-Westbourne boundary thus becomes a crevasse across Kensington Gardens into which some highly important context simply vanishes.

The eastward link with Hyde has long been known but its exact nature has never been explored and Hyde itself, always wrongly seen as a monolithic block, and the formation of Hyde Park have both therefore been seriously misunderstood. Knowing the initial extent of Hyde Park is also essential for understanding the formation of Kensington Palace and Gardens. Although in 1820 Kensington's great historian, Thomas Faulkner, started his lengthy coverage of the palace by stating that it 'takes its name from the adjoining town although it is situate in the parish of St Margaret's Westminster', he did

4   E. Walford, *London Old and New*, 5 (1878), 15; Chancellor, *Knightsbridge* is also highly but selectively derivative.
5   *Survey of London*, XLV, 1; Pevsner, *Westminster*, 727–58.
6   Impey, *Kensington Palace*, will be superseded by Fryman, *Kensington Palace*.
7   Impey, *Kensington Palace*, 11–12; Eye's boundaries are shown in the Frontispiece, iv–v.
8   See Map 2; for some of the meanings of vill see *VCH Middx*, XIII, 5.
9   Saunders, 'Extent of Westminster', 230–1, and plans I–III (unpag.); M. Gelling, 'The boundaries of the Westminster charters', *Trans. London & Middx Arch. Soc.*, n.s. 11 (1953), 101–4, was written in ignorance of Saunders's work and only considers Westminster's main block of land.

not realise the implications and most of his successors have been entirely unwilling to do so.[10]

Because Knightsbridge failed to become its own parish it remained a detached portion of Westminster, but historians of Westminster have understandably concentrated on their core area. This has led to some anomalies. Gervase Rosser's excellent *Medieval Westminster* was specifically limited to the vill but the statistics gleaned from St Margaret's parish records must, in fact, include Knightsbridge.[11] Julia Merritt's equally excellent studies of Westminster between 1525–1640 provide a stimulating exploration of Hyde Park as an area of elite sociability but slip out of focus on the western edges.[12] In her second volume, Knightsbridge (except as a general address for the lazarhouse) is treated as beyond Westminster and partly as a result Hyde Park is given exclusively to St Martin-in-the-Fields, and Kensington's Holland House placed just across the St Martin's border.[13] One of Merritt's major contributions is to show the importance of the Westminster dimension to the national picture, and Knightsbridge was very much part of this.

A full history of such a complex area would need a very long book, and this is a short one. Since its main aim is to fill gaps in previous knowledge it pays particular attention to the manor and the effects of the parks' creation, but there is plenty of other material to draw a wider picture. Initial scene-setting touches on the geology and road structure, and on the difficulties around Knightsbridge's intriguing place-name. The manorial records provide rich information on the vanished landscape and its agriculture. They are also an excellent resource for some of the early development of the settlement and its economy, and since the court rolls continued down to 1793 they supplement the *Survey of London* descriptions of later development. New and old information is also woven together in a concluding account of the leper hospital and chapel that between the 15th and 17th centuries were Knightsbridge's most famous features.

The Early Background: Geology, Roads, Place-name

Geology

Knightsbridge and Hyde are within the Thames valley and all the land is well below 100 ft above mean sea level, albeit with a noticeable southward descent. Although the bedrock is London Clay it is mostly covered by parts of the two lower terraces of the Stage III drifts, or River Terrace Gravels, known as the Middle or Taplow Terrace and the Low or Flood Plain Terrace. The bluff that marks the boundary between them 'is a distinctly traceable feature in the topography of London, running from Holland Park past the Albert Hall to Knightsbridge, across the Green Park and along Jermyn Street to the river-bank at Trafalgar Square'.[14] The gravel meant that most of the soil was porous and well drained. At least in the early modern period the air was therefore considered

---

10   Faulkner, *Kensington*, 329.
11   Rosser, *Medieval W.*
12   Merritt, *W* (1), *W* (2).
13   Ibid., *W* (2), 8, 69, 215.
14   *VCH Middx*, I, 1–8, at 6 and with a geological map facing 2.

Figure 2 *St Govor's Well, Kensington Gardens. One of many springs across Knightsbridge and Hyde, it was named after the patron saint of Llandover in 1856 and received today's inscribed mounting in 1976.*

'pure and salubrious'.[15] There were major gravel pits on the Kensington/Knightsbridge border at Notting Hill before 1600.[16]

The non-porous clay is exposed in the valley formed by the river Westbourne, in the now-dry valley from a tributary spring that rises east of the river within Hyde Park, and along the boundary between the two river terraces.[17] The juncture of the gravel and clay gave rise to numerous springs and in consequence to water meadows, ditches and various conduits. For conduits see below, 50–1.

Roads[18]

Knightsbridge's eponymous bridge and hamlet were on the principal Roman road between London and the west, which runs from Ludgate along the Strand to Trafalgar Square before turning north up Haymarket to gain the bluff described above. The road then comes along Piccadilly to Hyde Park Corner (the park's south-eastern corner) and thence to Knightsbridge, Kensington and beyond, taking the straightest line above the river's extravagant curves. It was unfortunate that through Knightsbridge the road was on clay and therefore easily became 'a great impassable sea of mud'.[19] It usually features in Knightsbridge documents as the road to Brentford or Windsor but has been known more generally as the Bath Road, the Great West Road and, when roads were classified in the

15 Davis, *Knightsbridge*, 269–70.
16 TNA, C 54/1666 (1599); for early 17th-century references see below, 37, 40, 81.
17 OS geological sheets 256 and 270; for the geology within Hyde Park and Kensington Gardens, LUCHP and LUCKG.
18 Modern names are used throughout.
19 Lord Hervey, marooned in Kensington in 1736, quoted in Davis, *Knightsbridge*, 25.

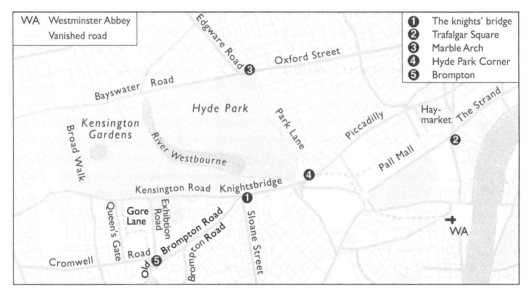

Map 1 *Map showing main roads mentioned in the text.*

1920s, the A4. Around 1960 this last designation was re-applied to the arterial route that diverges south-westward along the Brompton and Cromwell Roads.

The other Roman road heading west from London is Watling Street, which, having arrived from the south via London Bridge, leaves from Newgate then runs along Holborn and Oxford Street to Marble Arch, at Hyde Park's north-east corner. Here it turns north becoming today's Edgware Road or A5.[20] The westward continuation, also Roman and running along the top of the park towards Notting Hill, is usually referred to in the documents as the highway to Acton, Uxbridge or Oxford. This stretch is now the Bayswater Road and was part of the A40 until the 1930s creation of Western Avenue.[21]

These are the only three roads regularly called a royal road or king's highway in the medieval and early modern records, a term that was not applied to the local lanes, however useful their connective role. Brompton Road (only officially so-named along the whole of its current length in 1863 and until 1900 almost entirely in Kensington) ran from the Great West Road south-west to the important river crossing at Fulham (the lane to Brompton diverged west at 2016's Thurloe Place).[22] Cromwell Road was put through westward from Brompton Road in 1855 as part of the 1851 Commissioners' development of 'South Kensington' but did not span the railway until the 1930s or, after major works, become the replacement A4 until *c.*1960. Slightly further west Gore Lane, running directly down to Brompton, spanned the boundary until obliteration for 'South Kensington'. Its connective role passed to the new Queen's Gate, which in 1900 also became the borough boundary.

In the 1530s other roads vanished unmapped into Hyde Park but a degree of reconstruction is possible. A draft 1478 lease of the demesnes of Knightsbridge and Hyde

20   *VCH London*, I, 32–4.
21   http://www.sabre-roads.org.uk/wiki/index.php?title=A40/History (accessed 5 Feb. 2016).
22   For this and the following sentence, *Survey of London*, XXXVIII, 1–2.

mentions some minor field roads and two more major ones.[23] One of these ran from Oldway Gate on Windsor Way to Northway Gate on Acton Way and was presumably the *viam communem* called Oldeway whose obstruction was reported in 1443.[24] It is perhaps possible that the Broad Walk across Kensington Gardens, which links the lanes now disguised as Queensway (in Westbourne) and Palace Gate/Gloucester Road (Kensington), reflects this Knightsbridge section of a previous through-route, although judging from the boundary of the eventual Hyde Park, today's Broad Walk was pretty much at the demesnes' western edge, and later demesne leases only give more general permission for passage 'through the roads of the manor(s)'.[25]

The other significant road ran past Cresswellshot alias Homefield, which was partly bounded on the north by Galowcroft (whose name came from the Tyburn gallows at Marble Arch) and on the east by 'a certain road which leads towards Hodilston(es)pitt(es)'.[26] This is slightly ahead of the better-known reference in 1483/5 to 'a lane called Westmynster lane, leading between Tyburn and lez Osilston Pyttes'.[27] The road is Park Lane, previously Westminster Lane and/or Tyburn Lane, which runs along the eastern side of Hyde Park and whose history is very obscure.[28] Before the southward continuation was severed in the 17th century by Green Park, the route carried on below Hyde Park Corner before turning east and soon forking, with one branch going towards Westminster and the other to Trafalgar Square via the road whose remnant survives as Pall Mall.

Park Lane is often said to be the southward continuation of Watling Street but even if this was so before the Romans established London and its river crossing, it has never been so since. Although it directly links the three Roman roads described above it was usually only called a lane, and even in 1478 when it was termed a road, unlike the roads to Windsor and Acton it was not a royal one.[29] Overestimating its importance has led to other misunderstandings, particularly the belief that the offset junction with the Edgware Road (at Marble Arch) needs an explanation. The one produced by Gatty, and still often cited, is that the lane provided the eastern boundary of the manor of Hyde, and that when Henry VIII added some adjacent land on the east, notably Stonehill, to create Hyde Park he moved the lane to form the new boundary.[30] But the 1478 description shows that Hyde was not a solid block and that Stonehill and the lane were both part of its eastern edge. Park Lane was widened to dual carriageway in the 1960s by taking in part of the park.[31]

23 WAM, 4870, see Appendix, 77–80, which gives the varying original spellings.

24 WAM, 16448 m.1

25 WAM, Reg. Bk I f. 33v (1488): *per vias maneriorum*; Reg. Bk II ff. 163v–164 (1520): *per vias manerii*.

26 On the spelling see Appendix, 79; on the gallows see London CC (G.L. Gomme), *Tyburn Gallows* (1909).

27 Gatty, *Mary Davies*, I, 58–9; for Ossulston see below, passim.

28 It was still Tyburn Lane in 18th-century documents e.g. WAM, 24894–909, 52262–3; on the chronology of the names see Davis, 'Conduit System', 39.

29 It was called a king's highway in 1740 (WAM, 24894) but that is probably too late to count. For the lane as Watling Street's southern extension see the maps in Davis, 'Conduit System', 54, 56.

30 Gatty, *Mary Davies*, I, 32–3; the idea is there in embryo in Davis, 'Conduit System'; later citations include LUCHP, 9.

31 LUCHP, 22.

Place-name

Knightsbridge first appears, as Cnihtebricge, in Edward the Confessor's alleged confirmation of Westminster Abbey's estates given at Christmas 1065.[32] Since it is not mentioned in Domesday Book the first totally reliable reference comes in the 1130s, this time as Cnithtebruga, and other medieval references also consistently deploy forms of Old English *cniht-* and Middle English (and modern) knight-.[33] Despite this, the mistaken 19th-century antiquarian belief that the name derived from King is still sometimes repeated.[34]

The bridge element is easy: the bridge carried the Great West Road across the river Westbourne at today's Albert Gate.[35] The *cnihtas*, though, are deeply obscure.[36] *Cniht* initially meant young man, servant, follower, so in theory the bridge could have become known as the meeting spot for the local lads, but in fact this is highly unlikely because the term rapidly both climbed the social scale and became attached to significant urban groups. There was a group or guild of *cnihtas* in mid 9th-century Canterbury, and in early 11th-century Cambridge *cnihtas* were associated with a thegns' guild concerned with peacekeeping. The best-known *cnihtengilda* was the one in London whose rights as in the days of Kings Edgar (d. 975), Æthelred and Cnut were confirmed by Edward the Confessor in 1042x1044, and it seems likely that these *cnihtas* started as servants appointed by the city's property-owing magnates to provide them with goods from the local markets, but then either became or were joined by people with independent trading status.[37]

The only land firmly associated with the London *cnihtengilda* is the later Portsoken ward, immediately east of the City walls and transferred in 1125 to Holy Trinity Priory Aldgate, but this was land that they actually possessed.[38] Like the other town guilds the London *cnihtengilda* probably had a considerably wider territorial remit, whether for provisioning, peacekeeping or both, but if the bridge was somehow connected to the guild, then in what capacity is entirely unclear. The suggestion of a western guild to match the eastern one, made in 1906, looks unlikely in the light of later research into the guilds' economic function, and Knightsbridge is obviously quite a long way from the City.[39] If the London guild did ever operate across a wide zone it must, like the London Peace Guild of the 930s, have acted irrespective of estate boundaries, and its role had probably in any case dwindled well before Westminster Abbey acquired Knightsbridge.[40]

---

32   WAM, WD f. 45, S1039.
33   Mason, *WA Charters*, no. 250; *PN Middx* (EPNS), 169.
34   For example: *Survey of London*, XLV, 4; Pevsner, *Westminster*, 755.
35   See below, Maps 6 and 8.
36   This whole section is deeply indebted to Keene, 'Knights'.
37   F.M. Stenton, 'Norman London', in D.M. Stenton (ed.), *Preparatory to Anglo-Saxon England* (Oxford, 1970), 32–3, expanded by Keene, 'Knights', 201–2.
38   Keene, 'Knights', 202–3.
39   W.F. Prideaux, 'Notes on Salway's Plan of the Road from Hyde Park Corner to Counter's Bridge', *London Topographical Soc. Rec.* 3 (1906), 24.
40   On the Peace Guild see P. Taylor, 'Boundaries and Margins: Barnet, Finchley and Totteridge', in M.J. Franklin and C. Harper-Bill (eds), *Medieval Ecclesiastical Studies in Honour of Dorothy M. Owen* (1995), 277–8.

Knightsbridge almost certainly came to the abbey in 998x1065 and it was still part of Westminster manor in 1086. By then the manor was housing 25 *milites* – soldiers or knights, the Latin translation of *cnihtas* – but these cannot have been relevant to the bridge or its name. The bridge was on the boundary between Knightsbridge and Eye, which lay on the east and separated the main block of Westminster from its detached area. On the eve of the Norman Conquest, Eye was held in royal trusteeship for the underage son of Earl Ralph of Hereford and after the Conquest it was given briefly to William the Chamberlain and then in the early 1080s to Geoffrey de Mandeville, who passed it to the abbey shortly before his death *c.*1097. So this was not a boundary that either side in 1086 needed to defend. And although it could perhaps be argued that Knightsbridge's southern boundary seems designed to include, and therefore potentially protect, the main road along the stretch from the bridge to Gore, westward from Gore and still between the same manors, Knightsbridge/Westminster and Kensington, the boundary was along the centre of the road.

Knowing the boundaries is also important in evaluating some later medieval references which suggest links between London and Knightsbridge. In 1257 when Henry III was returning eastward 'towards Westminster, the mayor and citizens went according to custom to greet him at Kniwtebrigge'.[41] This seems to be a unique reference, perhaps recorded because the king refused to meet them, but comparable ceremonies are recorded at Southwark's southernmost tip at St Thomas à Watering on the Old Kent Road, the equivalent southern road from London. All such ceremonies here, though, would surely have occurred at Knightsbridge/Westminster's western edge, most probably at Gore, not at the eastern bridge. In the later 14th century, there were City edicts forbidding the butchering of animals anywhere nearer than Knightsbridge, Stratford and suchlike distant places, but these were attempted health measures, not a formal link.[42]

---

41   *De Antiquis Legibus Liber*, Camden Soc., 31 (1846), cited in Davis, *Knightsbridge*, 25–6.

42   Davis, *Knightsbridge*, 32–3 (1361); Chancellor, *Knightsbridge*, 7 (1371, 1379/80).

Manor, Parish and Liberty

Knightsbridge in Relation to Westminster, Westbourne and Paddington

KNIGHTSBRIDGE'S INITIAL RELATIONSHIP TO Westminster, Westbourne and Paddington has never previously been explored, but it was absolutely crucial for most of its later history.

Because Westminster Abbey forged so many of its title deeds in the 12th century, almost all its supposedly pre-Conquest documents have to be treated with great caution.[1] Nevertheless it is virtually certain that the block of land containing Knightsbridge, Westbourne and Paddington had come to the abbey before 1066, and in at least two stages. The first reference to any of the three places comes in King Edgar's alleged confirmation in 959 of estates that included Paddington, but this document is deeply untrustworthy.[2] Some of the confected charters, though, clearly include genuine material and one of these is Æthelred II's alleged confirmation of estates c.998, where the list ends with three that were promised as reversions – transfer once the existing incumbent died and a term used equally for resumptions and new acquisitions.[3] One of these reversions was Paddington, a *praediolum* or small estate in the hands of a life tenant named Wulfric, and that it was conspicuously small suggests that the western boundary, then as later, was the river Westbourne. The eventual Paddington parish was roughly twice as large because it also included Westbourne.

Westbourne is not mentioned by name until 1222 and in all subsequent documents was part of Knightsbridge manor. Knightsbridge itself appears in only one of the abbey's supposedly pre-Conquest confirmations, Edward the Confessor's *Telligraphus* issued at Christmas 1065. This too probably contains authentic material, which makes it interesting that Knightsbridge is given four hides to Paddington's two; since Knightsbridge by itself was also small, this suggests it already included Westbourne.[4]

Even without relying on the confirmations there is a very strong reason to accept that the abbey had acquired the whole of the Paddington–Knightsbridge–Westbourne

1   R. Mortimer's *Charters of Westminster Abbey* (Brit. Acad. Charters Series, forthcoming) is eagerly awaited.
2   S 1293; M. Gelling, *The Early Charters of the Thames Valley* (1979), no. 221.
3   S 894; M. Gelling, *Charters*, no. 231; Sullivan, *W Corridor*, 112–13; Simon Keynes, 'Wulfsige, monk of Glastonbury, abbot of Westminster (c.990–3), and bishop of Sherborne (c.993–1002)', in K. Barker *et al* (eds), *St Wulfsige and Sherborne: Essays to Celebrate the Millennium of the Benedictine Abbey 998–1008*, Bournemouth Univ. Sch. of Conservation Science Occasional Paper 8 (2005), 56–9.
4   S 1039; unpub. MSS: WAM, WD ff. 43–45v; BL, Cotton Faustina ff. 113v–120. F.E. Harmer, *Anglo-Saxon Writs* (1952), 289–92; Sullivan, *W Corridor*, 71, 113; Harvey, *WA Estates*, 353.

Figure 3 *St Margaret's was built next to the abbey, on part of the monks' burial ground. The proximity is captured in 'The East Prospect of the Abby of St. Peter & of the Parish Church of St. Margaret, Westminster',* c.*1720.*

block before 1066, and this is the block's unique relationship with the home Westminster manor and parish. In 1222 these three places alone formed a detached portion of St Margaret's parish and this fits with the evidence in Domesday Book (1086), where Westminster manor is assessed at an otherwise high 13½ hides and Paddington and Knightsbridge are unnamed. If they had been in other hands they would have had their own entries, like neighbouring Eye, Kensington, and Chelsea.[5]

In the century or so after 1086 Paddington and Knightsbridge were both separated from the home manor. Paddington was assigned to the abbey almoner at the start of the 12th century.[6] Knightsbridge was a separate manor by the 1130s when abbot Herbert granted land in Gore *in tenetura manerii nostri de Cnithtebruga.*[7] In 1157 a list of the abbey's Middlesex estates starts: vill of Westminster, Knightsbridge, Paddington, Totehal, vill of Eye.[8] But separation from the home manor did not entail separation from the home parish and in 1222 Knightsbridge, Westbourne, and Paddington including its chapel were all still part of St Margaret's parish.

---

5   GDB, f. 128b, 4.1; 129c, 9.1; 130d, 21.1; 130c–d, 20.1 (*Domesday*, 366); Harvey, *WA Estates*, 350 n. 4, makes a rare mistake in saying that Eye is not mentioned.

6   Harvey, *Obedientiaries*, xxiv.

7   Mason, *W Charters*, no. 250. For Gore, see below, 20–3.

8   Papal confirmation, WAM, WD f. 3b.

The parishioners worshipped in the abbey until they were transferred to their own adjacent church, dedicated to St Margaret of Antioch and probably new when first recorded in 1121x1136, although a 14th-century abbey tradition attributed its foundation to Edward the Confessor.[9] Either way the parish's tithes had been awarded to the almoner of Westminster by *c.*1083, which suggests the unit had a pre-Conquest definition, and the almoners were subsequently *ex officio* rectors of St Margaret's.[10] It was still sometimes described as a chapel into the 1190s, although by then it had given its name to the parish and disputes about exemption from diocesan control were well underway.[11]

These disputes were finally settled in 1222 by papal judges delegate headed by Archbishop Stephen Langton, and they awarded the abbey an ecclesiastical liberty entirely exempt from diocesan or other intervention.[12] This liberty was specifically limited to the abbey precinct and St Margaret's parish, which is therefore described. The main block reached west to the Tyburn and north to Oxford Street but the parish included a detached portion containing the vills of Knightsbridge, Westbourne and Paddington and a chapel at Paddington. Crucially this means that the manor of Eye, which bridged the gap between the main parish block and Knightsbridge and had come to the abbey *c.*1097, had not been assigned to St Margaret's, and it is this contrast that strengthens the evidence that Knightsbridge, Westbourne and Paddington constituted St Margaret Detached because they had been within the pre-Conquest home manor.[13]

Paddington's chapel seems to have been upgraded to a parish church by the 1320s, when Thomas de Cherlecote was witnessing as vicar.[14] The parish was almost certainly then still limited to Paddington manor, and in 1330 Westbourne was firmly termed a hamlet of Knightsbridge, which, given that Knightsbridge itself remained a hamlet, shakes the usual understanding of the term.[15] By 1452, however, there is a reference to land in Dawberyshot in Westbourne as lying in the parish of Paddington.[16] Westbourne's residents were probably pleased to make the shorter journey but manorially Westbourne stayed in Knightsbridge. For residents in Knightsbridge proper, Paddington church was no closer than St Margaret's, and they were not transferred. But neither were they given their own chapel: despite the reference to tithes of fleeces from Knightsbridge in 1361/2 which led Barbara Harvey to assume one, this is an occasion when argument from the silence of every other source that lists the abbey's churches and chapels seems justified.[17] Residents eventually used the chapel attached to the leper hospital founded just east of the bridge in the 1460s.[18]

9   *VCH Middx*, XIII, 123–4; Rosser, *Medieval W*, 251–2.
10   Rosser, *Medieval W*, 252.
11   *VCH Middx*, XIII, 124.
12   K. Major (ed.), *Acta Stephani Langton Cantuariensis Archiepiscopi AD 1207–1228*, Canterbury & York Society 50 (1950), no. 54; *VCH Middx*, XIII, 4, 123.
13   See Frontispiece, iv–v.
14   *VCH Middx*, IX, 252–4; additionally, Thomas was vicar by 1323 and dead by 1334 and his church, later St Mary's, was described as St Nicholas at Paddington *iuxta* Kilburn: WAM, Liber Niger, nos CXXVIII–CXXIX.
15   WAM, WD ff. 113–113v.
16   WAM, 16335.
17   WAM, 18988; Harvey, *Obedientiaries*, 22, and pers. comm.
18   See Religious History, 67–73.

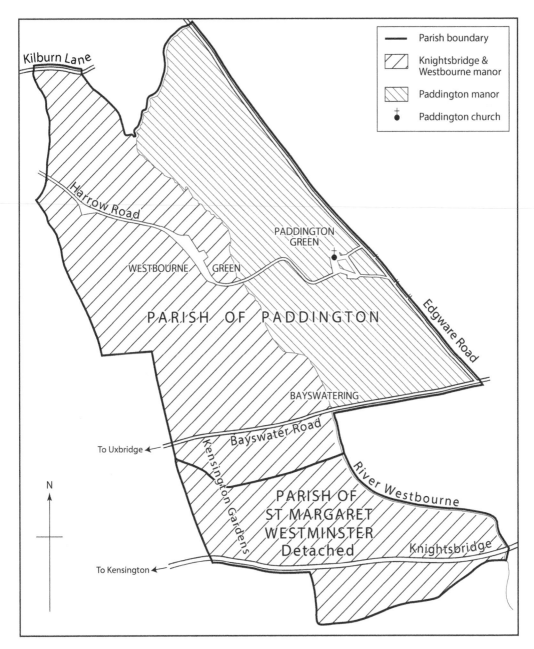

Map 2 *The relationship of the manors of Knightsbridge & Westbourne and Paddington to the parishes of St Margaret Westminster Detached and Paddington.*

The lack of a chapel capable of evolving into a parish church had a whole range of more or less predictable results, but one major consequence was entirely unexpected. When Paddington became a parish it was no longer part of St Margaret's, so by, at latest, 1452 all that was left of St Margaret Detached was the Knightsbridge part of Knightsbridge & Westbourne manor. Then in 1540, when Henry VIII dissolved Westminster Abbey and created the 'City of Westminster', this city was restricted to St Margaret's parish although the rest of Westminster, primarily the parish of St Martin-in-the-Fields – and therefore, for the first time, Eye – was also included by the phrase 'the City and Liberties (eventually the City and Liberty) of Westminster'.[19]

So Knightsbridge became the only one of the original trio to fall within the new City and Liberties, whose boundaries remained unaltered from 1540 until revisions under the London Government Act of 1899. That is why the boundaries of the Knightsbridge part of Knightsbridge & Westbourne manor, often treated as lost, are very easily found on Ordnance Survey and other pre-1900 maps, perfectly preserved as those of St Margaret (from 1888 St Margaret and St John the Evangelist) Westminster Detached.[20] Temporary add-ons such as the meadow at Chelsea sometimes rented in the 14th century did not affect the core manor.[21] It has also been said that Knightsbridge 'extended into the vills of Littleton, Paddington, and Westbourne'.[22] But the only permanent link was with Westbourne; Paddington, as we have seen, went its separate way and in 1330 the abbot specifically denied having any property in Littleton, better known as Lisson, a non-abbey manor east of Paddington that became part of Marylebone parish.[23]

Westminster Abbey survived the Reformation, albeit in modified form, and retained Knightsbridge & Westbourne manor, but it lost Paddington. When the monks surrendered to the Crown, on 16 January 1540, all the abbey's estates passed into the court of augmentations.[24] On 17 December 1540, Henry VIII created both the City of Westminster and a bishopric of Westminster with the abbey as its cathedral and a named bishop, dean (the former abbot) and canons. The bishop's landed endowment was transferred to him on 21 January 1541 but the dean and chapter's took until 5 August 1542.[25] The abbey's previous endowment was not completely restored and among the losses was Paddington. When the bishopric was wound up in 1550 the dean and chapter's

19   *VCH Middx*, XIII, 5; at 2 it forgets Knightsbridge in stating that the river Westbourne formed the western edge of the City of Westminster as well as the vill of Eye. For Westminster's unsuccessful 16th- and 17th-century attempts at incorporation, as well as examples of the shift in usage to City and Liberty, Merritt, *W (1)* and *W (2)*.

20   See especially *Old OS Maps*, London 60 (1872, 1893), 61 (1870, 1894), 74 (1871, 1894), 75 (1869, 1894); on the parish amalgamation: *VCH Middx*, XIII, 8.

21   See Agriculture, 47.

22   Harvey, *WA Estates*, 353.

23   WAM, WD ff. 113–113v.

24   On the surrender see B. Harvey, 'The Dissolution and Westminster Abbey', http://www.monlib.org.uk/papers/westminster/2007harvey.html (accessed 13 Oct. 2015). For the rest of this section, C.S. Knighton, 'Introduction' and 'King's College' in C.S. Knighton and R. Mortimer (eds), *Westminster Abbey Reformed 1540–1640* (2003), 1–37; C.S. Knighton, 'Collegiate foundations, 1540–1570, with special reference to St Peter in Westminster', Cambridge Ph.D thesis, 1975.

25   The statement in *VCH Middx*, IX, 229 that Knightsbridge with Westbourne was granted in 1542 to the short-lived see, from which it passed to the dean and chapter of the collegiate church, is not quite accurate.

Figure 4 *The course of the river Westbourne in the stretch below the dam.*

endowment survived intact but the bishop's passed to the bishopric of London along with some other estates, among them Paddington.[26]

Knightsbridge's Boundaries

Perambulating the bounds, a time-honoured tradition, will include looking at some deep-seated oddities at Bayswater and Gore, at 'South Kensington', and at the borough boundary changes of 1900 and 1965. Knightsbridge's only natural boundary was the eastern one formed by the river Westbourne, which separated Knightsbridge, Chelsea and the southernmost strip of Westbourne from Eye and the rest of Westbourne from Paddington. The river rises in Hampstead and runs south to the Thames and its current name is a 19th-century back formation from the adjacent place-name, which itself means 'west of the river'.[27] In medieval documents it is usually simply the river or rivulet (*rivulus*), sometimes qualified as of or next to (*iuxta*) Knightsbridge,[28] or the ditch (*fossat'*) called Bayard's Watering.[29] The section across Hyde Park/Kensington Gardens was broadened and transformed in the early 18th century into the Long Water and Serpentine. In the 1860s, because of worsening pollution, this part of the river was diverted into London's new sewerage system and since then the Long Water and

26   *Cal. Pat.* 1549–51, 262; *VCH Middx*, IX, 226.
27   *PN Middx* (EPNS), 8.
28   For example, WAM, WD f. 107v. (1297), 16238 (1319).
29   WAM, 16187 (1376) Bayhardeswa[tery]ng.

Figure 5 *Boundary stones at the top of the Long Water separating the parish of St George Hanover Square (created in 1725 from the Eye part of St Martin-in-the-Fields), from Paddington parish and Metropolitan Borough.*

Serpentine have been fed from other sources.[30] The above-ground channel between the dam and Albert Gate only carries overflow water but it follows the river's original course. The Knightsbridge stretch has remained a parish boundary but has not been a demarcation for either the Metropolitan or the London Borough of Westminster, which descend from the City and Liberties.

The northern boundary separated Knightsbridge from Westbourne and also therefore Westminster Detached from Paddington. It ran from the river west to Kensington and if it had utilised the main road it too would have been straightforward. Instead, Oxford Street/Bayswater Road, which between London and the Westbourne provided a continuous run of boundaries for Westminster, Eye and Paddington, was abandoned at the river for a line that runs some 1,000 ft further south. This is the more remarkable because the field or shot (a sub-division) with the interesting name of Halfhyde straddled the boundary.[31]

Abandoning such a road is so unusual that an early unit centred on Bayard's Watering perhaps becomes worth considering, even though the only obvious explanation for

---

30   *VCH Middx*, IX, 246–7; N. Barton and S. Myers, *The Lost Rivers of London* (revised edn., 2016), 78, 82–3, 195–6.
31   A court roll entry in 1518 carefully distinguishes parts of Halfhyde in the two parishes: WAM, 16449.

its existence is demonstrably wrong. The name Bayard's Watering, attested from 1376, though usually in terms of the river, has morphed through Bayswatering into Bayswater, but on pre-19th-century maps this was simply a hamlet immediately north of the road and west of the river.[32] It has sometimes been assumed that the name derives from Bainiardus (Baynard) who was holding abbey land assessed at three hides in Westminster in 1086, and that this was Ralph Baynard, the major Domesday landholder entrusted with the construction of Baynard's Castle on the City of London's western edge.[33]

Unfortunately neither assumption is valid. The place-name forms are from Bayard, not Baynard.[34] And the grant behind the Domesday holding was made in the 1080s to William Baynard and was of 'a certain berewic (outlying portion) of the vill of Westminster called *Totenhala*'.[35] This can be identified as the berewic purchased from King Æthelred in 1002 and both the term and the Domesday detail of a well-wooded holding strongly suggest that it was Tottenhall at Holborn rather than Tothill near the abbey – which makes a supplement from Westbourne even less plausible.[36]

Whatever the original rationale, it was the boundary's oddity that eventually placed this one small southern section of Westbourne, and with it Paddington parish, into what became Hyde Park and Kensington Gardens. Leases in 1378 for arable land in Halfhyde in Westbourne abutting north on the London to Oxford road show that the boundary was in place long before the park.[37] Although Knightsbridge and Westbourne formed a single manor whose jurors often made joint presentments, they were separate tithings with separate jurors and separate contributions to the common fine, and tithings, which long predated the 14th century, required fixed boundaries.[38]

Royal parks of the 16th century removed manor and parish rights (as did Kensington Gardens later) but the boundary line was jealously preserved. In 1656/7 the inhabitants of St Margaret's and Paddington met several times to 'reconcile the differences concerning the Boundes' and in 1658 boundary stones between St Margaret's, Paddington and Kensington were ordered to be placed in the park.[39] In 1900 the western end of the line was absorbed into the new Metropolitan Borough of Kensington but the rest was unaffected. In 1965 when the Metropolitan boroughs were in turn replaced by larger London boroughs this new version of the City of Westminster absorbed the Metropolitan Borough of Paddington, thus regaining the parish of Paddington, including Westbourne, forgone some half a millennium earlier.

Knightsbridge/Westminster's western boundary was entirely with Kensington. Until 1900 the line ran south from just below Bayswater Road to the Great West Road, where

32   In WAM, 16187 as Bayhardeswa[tery]ng; this is slightly earlier than the first example given in *PN Middx* (EPNS), 132–3. For maps see *VCH Middx*, IX, 180–4.

33   GDB 128b, 4.1–2 (*Domesday*, 361); R. Mortimer, 'The Baynards of Baynards Castle', in C. Harper-Bill *et al* (eds), *Studies in Medieval History presented to R. Allen Brown* (Woodbridge, 1989), 241–53, makes the link to Ralph at 243.

34   *PN Middx* (EPNS), 132–3 citing mainly 17th-century sources. The medieval sources concur.

35   WAM, WD f. 82, inserted in a 15th-century hand. Printed in Robinson, *Gilbert Crispin*, 38; discussed in *VCH Middx*, XIII, 30; Sullivan, *W Corridor*, 80–1, 136; Rosser, *Medieval W*, 252.

36   S 903; S 1039; *VCH Middx*, XIII, 30; Sullivan, *W Corridor*, 80–1; Rosser, *Medieval W*, 252.

37   WAM, 16344; 16358.

38   There are clear references in WAM, 16447 to separate homage juries (for the ordinary courts) in 1380 and capital pledges (for the views of frankpledge) in 1408.

39   WCA, E 36, cited in Merritt, *W (2)*, 250; *VCH Middx*, IX, 173.

Figure 6 *The east front of Kensington Palace with the statue of Queen Victoria unveiled in 1893.*

it turned east to Gore. This stretch had no obvious natural features but in today's terms it ran immediately west of Palace Gardens.[40] The reasons why Kensington Palace and Gardens were almost entirely in Knightsbridge are explored in detail below but by 1900 were long forgotten. Kensington had become the Court Suburb and although no reigning monarch since George II had lived at the palace, Victoria had been born and brought up there. From the moment of her accession she deliberately never returned, but it was probably an intended tribute that a special provision was inserted into the 1899 London Government Act. Alongside general enquiries into boundary rationalisations must be a specific enquiry into transferring Kensington Palace to Kensington.[41]

The enquiry proceedings give some splendid examples of the gap between perception and historical reality. Kensington Vestry laid claim to the whole of Kensington Gardens, its barrister referring to 'a very fitting opportunity for a very great anomaly being

40   *Old OS Maps*, London 60 (1872, 1893); 74 (1871, 1894).
41   62 & 63 Victoria c. 14, section 21.

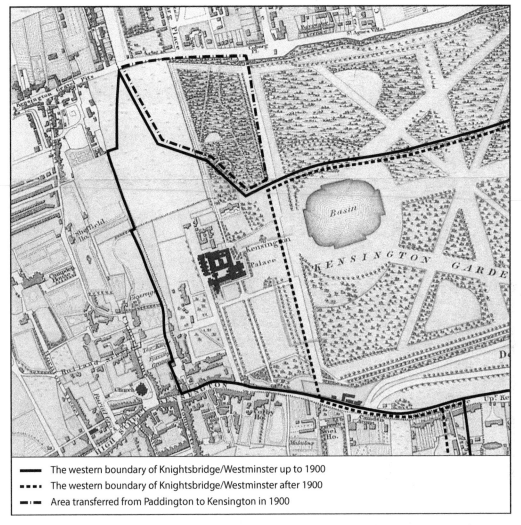

The western boundary of Knightsbridge/Westminster up to 1900
The western boundary of Knightsbridge/Westminster after 1900
Area transferred from Paddington to Kensington in 1900

Map 3 *The western boundary of Knightsbridge/Westminster with Paddington and Kensington pre- and post-1900, overlaid onto Greenwood's Map of London, 1827.*

adjusted, and for what is historically and topographically Kensington being constituted part of that borough'. Repeatedly challenged by Westminster's barrister – 'When you say a thing is historical you generally mean it is in accordance with fact' – he countered: 'if you want a history of Kensington Palace you do not find it in the historian's work on Westminster but you do find it in the historian's work on Kensington … all parties generally have recognised Kensington Palace as being situate in Kensington'; and when pushed again on 'historical fact' he responded 'if you will drop the word "historical" I will admit that it is a fact that it is situate in the parish of St John (sic), Westminster'.[42] Since parishes were the issue only Westminster, not Knightsbridge, was being considered, and no one did any serious research, but that undeniable fact helped achieve a compromise.

42   *LGA 1899*, 7, 13.

Figure 7 *Exhibition Road, looking north past Prince Consort Road. This section of 'South Kensington' is in Westminster/Knightsbridge.*

The new Metropolitan (from 1901, in another major victory, Royal) Borough of Kensington was extended east but only as far as the Broad Walk, leaving the rest of the parks between there and the river with Westminster/Knightsbridge and Paddington/Westbourne.[43]

Below the parks the pre-1900 boundary went east along the centre of the main road to Gore, where it again turned south. Gore means wedge and until obliterated in the 1850s for 'South Kensington' this was a wedge of land narrowing southward from the road. Gore Lane (also sometimes called Park Lane) ran through it and a significant hamlet extended down the lane from the road junction.[44] The boundary bisected the gore but ran east of the top part of the lane and the hamlet, putting them both in Kensington. The name survives today only in Kensington Gore, the stretch of the main road above the Albert Hall, but this is another unwarranted appropriation. Wasteland at a junction along a king's highway was generally considered royal land and an enquiry in 1270 found that 3 a. called King's Gore 'between Knightsbridge and Kensington'

43   *Old OS Maps*, London 60 (1914); 74 (1914).
44   There are published pre-obliteration maps in Faulkner, *Kensington* and *Survey of London*, XXXVIII, 53. The top of Jay Mews follows the top of Gore Lane.

Figure 8 *The Albert Memorial (1872) and 'Kensington Gore' (1879) are both, as the street sign indicates, in Westminster/ Knightsbridge.*

were ancient Crown demesne and the issues of 12*d.* per acre were paid to the sheriff of Middlesex.[45] In Knightsbridge manor records an area which considerably exceeded 3 a. was consistently called King's Gore until at least the 1770s.[46] Davis (1859), having shown it was 'originally called Kyngesgore', says that the area from 'Prince Albert's Road to Noel House is now generally considered as the Gore'; but this stretch, in modern terms running from Queen's Gate to Palace Gate, had always been well west of Gore Lane and Knightsbridge.[47] He does, however, also describe 'a row of five houses called emphatically Kensington Gore', lying close to Gore House and therefore east of the boundary.[48]

---

45 *Cal. Inq. Misc.* I, 126, cited in Davis, *Knightsbridge*, 11–12.
46 For example, WAM, 16444 (1400–3), 16453 m. 14 (1618), 52256 (1744–59), 16463 m. 2 (1771).
47 Davis, *Knightsbridge*, 131–2.
48 Ibid., 135–6; see also below, Settlement and Development, 62.

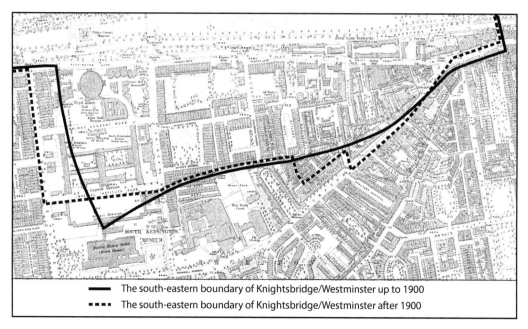

▬▬▬ The south-eastern boundary of Knightsbridge/Westminster up to 1900

▪▪▪▪ The south-eastern boundary of Knightsbridge/Westminster after 1900

Map 4 *The south-eastern boundary of Knightsbridge/Westminster pre- and post-1900.*

'Kensington Gore' appears below the developments on both sides of Gore Lane on various mid to late 18th-century maps and on Greenwood's map in both 1827 and 1854 Kensington Gore is marked above the development west of the boundary and Upper Kensington Gore east of it.[49] The 1871 25" OS survey still shows Upper and Lower Gore (sic) to either side of the Royal Albert Hall (which opened on 29 March) on Kensington Road; but in 1879 Kensington Gore was officially so-named and the surviving terraces correspondingly renamed and renumbered.[50]

There is no known sign of Crown interest after 1270 and no parish or manor gap 'between Knightsbridge and Kensington'. Knightsbridge certainly included at least part of Gore in the 1130s when abbot Herbert granted the nuns of Kilburn land to make a clearing in the manor of Knightsbridge in the place called Gara; the grant was confirmed by the next two abbots but vanishes thereafter.[51] Davis thought that the Gorefeld and Goremede listed among the convent's possessions in 1536 stemmed from it, but the wording clearly puts them in Kilburn and/or Paddington.[52] Despite later Knightsbridge manor references to property at or near the King's Gore there does seem to have been unusual uncertainty about the line at this point. St Margaret's parishioners perambulated the parish bounds regularly in the 1650s (as earlier) but in 1672 a report to Kensington manor stated that at a piece of land granted by Kensington's lord 'att the Kings Gore … the stones of the bounds were removed severall times and Westminster parish comes

49   See, for example, Cary, *New and Accurate Plan of London And Westminster*, 1795, http://mapco.net/
     cary1795/cary.htm (accessed 15 Mar. 2016). See also Map 3, above, 19 and Map 9, below, 59.

50   *Old OS Maps*, London 74 (1871, 1894); *Survey of London*, XXXVIII, 15.

51   *quandam terram ad sartandam*: Mason, *W Charters*, nos. 250, 265; WAM, Liber Niger ff. 125–125v,
     where this Gore section ends with the confirmation by abbot Lawrence (1158–73).

52   Davis, *Knightsbridge*, 14; 28 Henry VIII c. 38, *Statutes of the Realm*, III (1817), 695.

afterwards and Removes them again.'[53] Perhaps relatedly, the *Survey of London* noted minor anomalies between the manor and parish lines in the mid 19th century.[54]

The estate purchased by the 1851 Commissioners straddled the lines and therefore so too did the layout of 'South Kensington.'[55] The top of the boundary at Gore vanished under the Albert Hall and the subsequent stretch remained as an awkward angle that took in some two-thirds of the Imperial Institute (now Imperial College London) site. At the 1899 enquiry Westminster's share was readily acknowledged but the same points were raised about name recognition: 'popularly would I be right in saying that anybody would say the Albert Hall was in Kensington?' 'It is known as Kensington and all that portion is.' 'So with the Imperial Institute?' 'Yes.'[56] But there was no warrant for any general transfer and simple rationalisations were easily agreed. The southward line through Gore was moved west to the new Queen's Gate, and although it still continued east through today's Imperial College London, it did so on a straight line.

This line replaced the angle that had marked the last major turn along the southern boundary. Coming at last into the district now thought of as Knightsbridge, the line before 1900 ran north of the Brompton Road up to Knightsbridge Green, just below the junction with the main road, where it crossed over to run sequentially along both roads' southern verges, past an extruding tip of Kensington to the Chelsea boundary at the top of Sloane Street (a road put through in the 1770s). Here it dipped slightly further south before continuing to the river Westbourne. The 1900 rationalisation moved it to the centre of Brompton Road from Montpelier Street eastward, and kept it in the centre of the main Knightsbridge road along to the Westbourne.

Knightsbridge in Relation to Eye and Hyde

Having firmly located Knightsbridge as a manor entirely west of the Westbourne, it is time to complicate the picture by adding in the relationship with its eastern neighbour, Eye (also called Eia and Ebury), a solid block bounded by Oxford Street/Bayswater Road on the north and the rivers Tyburn, Westbourne and Thames on the east, west and south.[57] Until the mid 14th century Knightsbridge and Eye were completely separate entities which had come to the abbey at different times and were always in different parishes. Eye was given to the abbey by Geoffrey de Mandeville (the Domesday holder) *c.*1097 and was in St Martin-in-the-Fields's parish until assigned to the new St George Hanover Square in 1725.[58] Also when the abbey's estates were divided in 1225 Knightsbridge was assigned to the convent's portion and Eye to the abbot's.[59]

---

53 Paper in bundle TNA, E 192/16. For the St Margaret's perambulations, Merritt, *W (1)*, 208–12, *W (2)*, 250.
54 *Survey of London*, XXXVIII, 3.
55 Ibid., XXXVIII and below, Settlement and Development, 49, 61–3.
56 *LGA 1899*, 9–10.
57 See Frontispiece, iv–v. On Eye in general see *VCH Middx*, XIII, 32–6; Rutton, 'Manor of Eia'; Sullivan, *W Circle*.
58 GDB, f. 129v, 9.1 (*Domesday*, 363); Mason, *WA Charters*, no. 52. On the parish position see above and *VCH Middx*, XIII, 'Religious History'.
59 WAM, WD f. 629v; Harvey, *Obedientiaries*, xxv.

Nevertheless from the mid 14th century Knightsbridge was intermeshed with an adjacent part of north-west Eye known as Hyde. Hyde's own history is difficult and many previous assumptions are unfounded. Because a hide was notionally a unit of 100–120 a., it has been assumed that land let to Hugh de Kendale in 1258x1283 was identical with the 100-a. estate called la Hyde bought for the abbey from de Kendale's successors in 1350, and with the sub-manor of Hyde.[60] But there is plenty of evidence that even if an ur-unit of Hyde existed the de Kendale family were not granted all of it, and that they and their successors enlarged the estate before the abbey bought it in 1349/50. So even initially it was not an unchanging block, but something far more radical then followed. The abbey immediately put all of its new estate into demesne (direct ownership) and merged most of its administration with Knightsbridge, and the 'manor of Hyde', a term never used before its first lease (or farm) in 1358, was not the earlier Hyde but the combined demesnes of Hyde and of Knightsbridge between the two main roads. The detail to support all this is interesting in itself and raises useful questions about the meanings of both hide and manor, but it is particularly important because of the light it throws on the relationship between the manor of Hyde and Hyde Park.

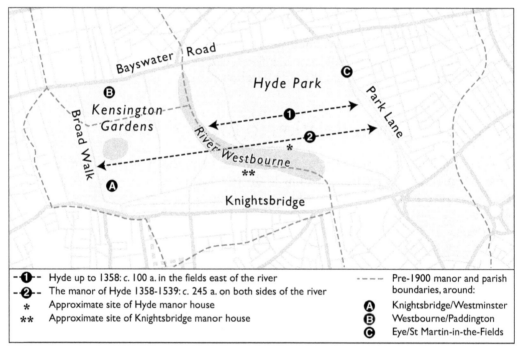

Map 5 *Historians have thought that Hyde comprised all of north-west Eye and have mapped it to match Hyde Park east of the river Westbourne. See, for instance, VCH Middx, XIII, Map 16. Hyde is in fact unmappable but the parameters can be shown. The original Hyde Park, whose western boundary was close to today's Broad Walk, covered 622 a.*

60   *VCH Middx*, XIII, 35–6, whose account starts with the de Kendales, and *PN Middx* (EPNS), 168–9.

The Descent of Hyde from the Early 13th to Mid 14th Centuries

The earliest known reference to Hyde comes in 1204 when John son of Firmin transferred 5 a. and a messuage 'in Hida' to John de Purtepole.[61] That 'in' might suggest a hamlet but there is no sign of one in any later documents and Eye was not divided into tithings, which argues against secondary settlements.[62] Hyde did, however, have a single significant house which, whether or not it was the one mentioned in 1204, belonged by the later 13th century to the de la Hyde family. Geoffrey de la Hyde appears in a (non-abbey) Westminster deed in 1257, but without an address.[63] Absolutely certainly, though, when John de la Hyde died, between December 1280 and May 1281, the Eybury reeve paid a boy to hold the house for six days, and later in 1281 sold the pasture from a ditch 'next to the court of John de la Hyde'.[64]

The star of the de Kendales was rising as that of the de la Hydes declined, but there was an overlap. The abbey's direct involvement with these incomers from 'Wadyngton' is first documented in 1285 but as a confirmation to Hugh and John de Kendale of land previously granted by abbot Richard (1258x1283) to Hugh for life.[65] At least up to John de la Hyde's death in 1280–1 the abbot's grant could not have included the house, and in any case the 1285 document is detailed and refers only to land. The land comprised two separated furlongs (*culturae*) 'in the field (*campo*) called Cressewellefeld and Osolueston' and two other 2-a. pieces; all were near the river (*torrentem*) and all abutted on lands belonging to other people. So not only was no house involved but the land was neither a solid block nor described as Hyde. Ossulston and Cresswell fields, under various spellings and usually as two fields rather than one, feature throughout the later documents.

A further 5 a. '*iuxta* la Hide' that the de Kendales purchased from William de Padynton in 1291, which abutted on their lands 'towards (*versus*) Mabilecroft', are presumably the 5 a. '*iuxta* la Hide' previously quitclaimed William by his mother and described as lying between land 'formerly of John de Hida' and land of Hugh de Kendale.[66] This again shows that the de Kendale estate was not a solid block and that 'Hyde' had a limited and different meaning, and it also again suggests that John de Hida, whether the father (d. 1280/1) or son (then a minor), was still in situ when the de Kendales began their accumulation. What happened to the de la Hydes is unclear. John 'son of John de la Hyde' witnessed abbey documents in 1298 and 1303 and also in 1298 successfully asserted his rights against his uncle and childhood guardian, Ralph the

61   W.J. Hardy and W. Page (eds), *A Calendar to the Feet of Fines for London and Middlesex,* 1: Richard I–Richard III (1892), John no. 29.

62   Eye accounts and court rolls: WAM, 26848–27008.

63   W.J. Hardy and W. Page (eds), *A Calendar to the Feet of Fines for London and Middlesex,* 1: Richard I–Richard III (1892), Henry III no. 381.

64   WAM, 26854: *in expensis i garcionis tenent' seys' ad domum Johannis de la Hyde per vi dies post mortem ipsius vi*d. I am grateful to Matthew Payne for confirming the reading. WAM, 26855: *iuxta curiam.*

65   WAM, 4875; they are described as 'de Wadyngton' in 1291: WAM, 4874. See *VCH Middx*, XIII, 35, although its account of Hyde starts with the de Kendales, and Sullivan, *W Circle*, 281–3, who gives useful detail although his understanding of the relative location of the de la Hyde and de Kendale estates is flawed.

66   WAM, 4874 (1291), 4881 (n.d.).

Vintner.[67] But by 1324 when John's widow claimed her dower from land in Rosamunds (elsewhere in Eye) with which her husband had enfeoffed John de Benstede in 1312, she stated that no other lands from which to satisfy the dower had descended to her husband's heirs.[68]

The de Kendales never achieved a total monopoly: in 1308 John le Rok bought 1 a. of arable in 'the field called Oseleston' abutting north on the main road and east and west on John de Kendale's lands and in 1312 sold it to Adam de Halliwell.[69] In 1315 John son of Hugh de Kendale transferred all his 'lands and tenements at La Hyde' to John de Pelham and his wife Denise.[70] The next year de Halliwell sold his acre to de Pelham, in a deed endorsed simply 'Osulton'.[71] The word Hyde was still not being applied to the fields in which the de Kendale/Pelham lands lay but the 'lands and tenements' transferred in 1315 must have included the de la Hyde house or its replacement since the holding was increasingly being identified as La Hyde and documents were being signed there. In 1341 the house was termed 'my messuage called le Hyde *iuxta* Knightsbridge' and other 1340s descriptions include 'lands and tenements in Eye', 'lands and tenements called la Hyde', and 'at La Hyde in Eye'.[72] 'Manor' was never used. In 1347 Denise de Pelham, long a widow, married John de Conuers, who already had local land, and when both succumbed to the Black Death their combined estate passed to Christine, wife of Peter de Alnmouth.[73] In 1349–50 nominees acting for Prior Litlyngton made two large purchases from the de Alnmouths: the Hyde estate, described as a messuage and 100 a. of land in Eye, and a further three messuages, 91 a. and 10s. 2d. quitrent in Knightsbridge, Kensington, Chelsea and Eye.[74] In 1354 the 'messuage and lands called la Hyde in Eye' were transferred directly to the abbey and so too, separately, were two of the three further messuages, the quitrent, and 48 a. in Knightsbridge and Eye, of which 28 a. lay in three named *culturae* in the field of Knightsbridge and 13 a. in 'the field of Eye in the *cultura* called Carswell field'.[75] In 1360, when the abbot granted rent charges against three properties to fund Prior Litlyngton's commemoration, the two that were local had become 'the manor of Hyde and 51 a. of land and 10s. 2d. quitrent formerly John Conuers' in the vill of Knightsbridge'.[76]

67   WAM, 4873; 16359 and WD f. 109; Sullivan, *W Circle*, 279–80.
68   *Cal. Inq. p.m.* VI, 287; *VCH Middx*, XIII, 95–6.
69   WAM, 4834, 4786.
70   WAM, 4871–2, 4879, 4883; for the transfer and more detail on the de Pelhams see *VCH Middx*, XIII, 35–6.
71   WAM, 4776. The description of this in *VCH Middx*, XIII, 36 as 'an acre in Eye called Ossulestone' is slightly misleading.
72   WAM, 16232, 4770, 4827, 4767.
73   *VCH Middx*, XIII, 36. For de Conuers' lands in La D(o)une and Shortelonds in 1272x1307 see WAM, 16201–3.
74   WAM, 4765. The Hyde transfer deed was made in Trinity term 1350 and this is the date that has always been cited, but Hyde was under direct abbey control from June 1349: WAM, 16431, see below. For the other purchase: WAM, 16209 with related documents from 1351–2, WAM, 16210, 16255, 16270, 16272. See also WAM, 5406, Liber Niger ff. 77, 101; Harvey, *W Estates*, 418–9.
75   Hyde: WAM, 4882, 4877; the other estate: WAM, 16180, 16212 (duplicates).
76   WAM, 5406.

The Abbey's Manor of Hyde

This 'manor of Hyde' had first appeared in April 1358 and was a totally new creation that covered not only the Hyde estate, all of which had been put into demesne (direct ownership), but also the adjacent demesnes in Knightsbridge. The choice of the single name for the manor, and therefore later for Hyde Park, has greatly confused the picture and has hidden Knightsbridge's contribution. At first, though, the boot was very much on the other foot and most of Hyde's administration was transferred to Knightsbridge.

This was initially done on a slightly ad hoc basis. In June 1349 Roger de Sudbury found himself *serviens* not only of Knightsbridge but also 'apud Hide', but in the following few years, costs at Hyde counted as foreign (i.e. external) expenses.[77] In 1352/3, though, Walter Leycester accounted as *serviens* of Knightsbridge and, on an attached sheet, as rector of Hyde, and by 1353/4 when he accounted solely as *serviens* of Knightsbridge but sowed grain in 'Hoselston' and 'Kersewell *iuxta* Hyde' (sic), the administration was fully integrated.[78] From here onwards too the accounts are indifferently headed Knightsbridge or Knightsbridge Hyde.

The last account in the run ends in April 1358, the month that the abbot gave the first lease of the demesnes and first deployed the phrase 'in manerio suo de la Hyde'.[79] Despite the single name this manor included two granges, 229 a. of arable and – the only field names supplied – 11 a. of meadow in Horsecroft and la More *iuxta* Kensyngton, the latter inescapably in Knightsbridge; an endorsement also gives 'E terris de Knyghtsbr' et La Hyde'.[80] The fields were later inclosed but the 1478 draft lease of 'the manor of Hyde' provides the name and abuttals of every close and shows definitively that the lands were at least as much west as east of the river and entirely between the two main roads; the Knightsbridge demesnes further south were not included.[81]

For a single farmer to maintain two closely adjacent farmhouses made little sense, and Knightsbridge's was lost. From 1474 the 'site of Knightsbridge manor' was let separately, and by 1520 it had become a close of 5½ a. 10 virgates, 'formerly called the manor of Knightsbridge'.[82] Since Knightsbridge manor and its courts continued unabated this shows that 'manor' and 'site of manor' could be used simply to refer to demesnes. A major unintended consequence was that when in 1536 Henry VIII removed all of Eye including 'the Manor of Hyde … now in the occupation of Thomas Arnolde' he also quietly gained a large part of Knightsbridge.[83] The rest only followed when the abbey was suppressed in 1540.

The relationship between the manor of Hyde and its two parent manors is all too easily confusing. The manor of Hyde was really only the farm of the demesne lands between the two main roads and any other entitlements and responsibilities were carefully defined. The last farm in 1520 was typical in excluding almost all the wood

---

77 WAM, 16431–2, 16436. The Eybury *serviens* changed in Apr. 1349, possibly because of the plague, but the accounts do not mention any other alteration: WAM, 26904–6.

78 WAM, 16437–8.

79 WAM, 16443, 16265.

80 La More straddled the Knightsbridge–Kensington border.

81 WAM, 4870, see Appendix, 77–80.

82 WAM, 16179, 16286, the latter also Reg. Bk II ff. 154v–155.

83 *L&P Henry VIII*, vol. XI, no. 202.

and absolutely all the regalities (royal powers vested in the lord of the manor including holding the views of frankpledge and the right to weyfs and strays).[84] So limited a sub-manor could never have superseded a main manor, but with Hyde there are a couple of complicating factors.

The first is the abbey's decision to treat the whole sub-manor of Hyde (whose lands lay slightly more in Knightsbridge than in Eye) as a single unit that was formally part of Eye but administratively part of Knightsbridge. Perhaps this was because since 1225 Eye had been part of the abbot's portion but because it was the prior who bought the Hyde estate (and in 1349/50 acted as its bailiff) it sat more easily with Knightsbridge, which was in the convent's share.[85] It must also have helped that there was no hamlet in Hyde, which would have strengthened the connection to the Eybury court. The formal link means that in 1398 Eybury's last extant court roll lists the sacristan's failure to attend court 'pro manerio le Hyde'.[86] Similarly in 1400–4 Knightsbridge's 'collector of the rents farms and [profits of the] court there' was responsible for transferring the assised rents (an archaic payment) from Hyde to Eybury, although this had in fact been done by the prior, apparently at that point again the recipient of the profits.[87] These profits had been transferred briefly to the cellarer in the 1360s and 70s and passed permanently to the warden of the new work c.1400.[88] In 1524x1536 the warden was still paying into Eybury the Hyde farmer's £14 plus 7s. [assised rents] 'for the manor of Hyde'.[89]

The other major complication is imprecise naming. The same unit was referred to as 'manor of Hyde' and, far less helpfully, 'manor of Knightsbridge and Hyde', 'manors of Knightsbridge and Hyde', 'manor of Knightsbridge' and 'manors of Knightsbridge'. Despite the patchy documentation, control of the manor of Hyde through Knightsbridge is easily shown. In 1368, while the Eybury court was definitely still meeting, Richard Ballard was summoned to the Knightsbridge court to answer for violations during his time as farmer 'apud La Hyde',[90] and in 1403/4 the Knightsbridge collector paid 'pro loppyng' various trees 'in la Grove de la Hyde'.[91] The warden of the new work could also be directly involved; in 1483/4 he paid 7s. for re-thatching a stable at Hyde, 40s. to its farmer for repairs and 'for his favour', and 7s. trying to limit the requisition of oats for the royal stable 'within the said manor'.[92] Proximity to the king's court always had serious disadvantages: in 1301/2 the Knightsbridge *serviens* was authorised to give royal officials 12d. not to cause damage in the manor.[93]

The nature of the farmers and to some extent the farms altered in line with wider trends. The initial grant in 1358 was to two local men for seven years and details the stock, the crops already sown, and the farmers' obligations to provide corn to

84   WAM, Reg. Bk II ff. 163v–4; WAM, 4880.
85   WAM, WD f. 629v; Harvey, *Obedientiaries*, xxv. For Prior Litlyngton as an administrator, see also Harvey, *WA Estates* (indexed as Litlington).
86   WAM, 27009.
87   WAM, 16444–5.
88   Harvey, *Obedientiaries*, 33, 118.
89   WAM, 43956.
90   WAM, 16446 m. 6.
91   WAM, 16445.
92   WAM, 23559; Rosser, *Medieval W*, 379.
93   WAM, 16390: *ministris regis ne facerent destructionem in manerio.*

the shepherd, cow-keeper and *famuli*.[94] By 1408 the farmer was John Croucher (or Crowcher), a citizen of London but almost certainly one with a strong local connection. A Lawrence Crowcher had a house and land in Knightsbridge in 1354.[95] Between 1375 and 1387, a John Croucher of Knightsbridge received several pavage (toll) grants towards repairing the London to Brentford road.[96] He also features in the court rolls of 1383–4 as both capital pledge and breaker of the assize of bread.[97] John Croucher, citizen and vintner, also appears in the patent rolls in 1410 and 1419 but only as someone to whom debts were owed.[98] In 1408 the manor jury provided a detailed report of the ruined state of 'the closes and buildings of the manors of Knightsbridge and le Hyde' let to Croucher, a situation he may well have inherited, but he had weakened a stable inside the moat by taking the roof tiles and re-using them on the external doorway.[99]

Croucher's co-operation with the main manor may have been exceptionally close. In 1412 he testified that an incoming freehold tenant had undertaken the requisite fine and fealty due to the abbot and convent;[100] and in 1440 the abbot and convent made a 20-year grant of a cottage and four closes in Knightsbridge to John Rawlyn of Westminster with the assent of John Croucher 'farmer of the manor of Knightsbridge'.[101] It is possible that his farm included more profits than usual: a 1417 rental 'of the manor of Hide *iuxta* Westminster' is actually a list of rents from lands and tenements elsewhere across Knightsbridge and Westbourne.[102]

In 1442 there was a change of tack with a 40-year lease of 'the manors of Knightsbridge' to the bishop of Salisbury, William Ayscough, whose active involvement is unlikely.[103] The lease (or farm) was at the highest known rent, 20 marks, and allegedly (and apparently uniquely) included 'the courts in the said manors' while exempting the other regalities and most of the wood. In fact, the farmer perhaps received the profits of the courts but rolls surviving from 1438–43 show no change. The abbey's annual view of frankpledge was still followed by the ordinary court, and the (new) farmer was among those presented for failing to scour ditches.[104] Ayscough was killed in 1450 during Cade's rebellion and who next took the farm is unclear, but in 1478 'the site of the manor of Hide' and all its appurtenances went to the bishop of Ely for 90 years.[105] The last farmers were rather more local, William Wallez, yeoman of Westminster (1487 and 1488) and from 1520 Thomas Arnold of Westminster, husbandman.[106] The 'site of Knightsbridge manor' was let separately from 1474 and although the farms of 1478 and 1520 refer only to the manor of Hyde they include the rest of the usual Knightsbridge lands. The texts of both the farms to Wallez grant the abbey's 'manor of Knightsbridge together with

94   WAM, 16265.
95   WAM, 16180, dupl. 16212.
96   *Cal. Pat.* 1375–77, 81, 124; 1377–81, 141, 605; 1381–5, 373; 1385–9, 328.
97   WAM, 16447, mm. 1, 8.
98   *Cal. Pat.* 1408–13, 249; 1416–22, 224.
99   WAM, 16447 m. 6–6v.
100 WAM, 16447 m. 4v.
101 WAM, 16448 m. 4v.
102 WAM, 16334, an undated later copy.
103 WAM, 16268.
104 WAM, 16448.
105 WAM, 4870, see Appendix, 77–80.
106 WAM, Reg. Bk I ff. 20–20v, 33v–34v; Reg. Bk II ff. 163v–164.

Figure 9 *The river Westbourne was widened across Hyde Park in the 1720s–30s to create the Long Water (shown here) and Serpentine. The result may have drowned the long-abandoned sites of either or both the Knightsbridge and Hyde manor houses.*

its manor of Hyde' but the marginal headings refer only to Knightsbridge (1487) and Hyde (1488). Since Wallez's grants specifically excluded regalities including the views of frankpledge, wood and a string of other extant farms, and carry no reference to anywhere north or south of the two main roads, this 'manor of Knightsbridge' can have been nothing more than the usual demesnes.

In 1535 Hyde was noted among Westminster Abbey's estates but Knightsbridge (apart from 10*s.* 11*d.* rents due to the Lady Chapel) was not, and this has understandably led to the suggestion that it was 'probably valued with Hyde'.[107] Yet Hyde's value was £14, which was only the annual farm. Perhaps the other income, including the known farm of the site of Knightsbridge manor, was subsumed into the total for Westminster.

Unfortunately no court rolls exist for Eybury beyond 1398 (though whether the court then ceased is unclear) while for Knightsbridge between 1358 and the loss of Hyde there are only patchy runs from 1358–1411, 1438–43 and 1511–29 plus a few extracts from

---

107 *Valor Eccl.*, I (1810), 413, 421; Harvey, *W Estates*, 353.

now-lost rolls made in the 1470s.[108] The 14th- and 15th-century entries are all titled Knightsbridge but by 1511 this has become Knightsbridge cum Westbourne.[109] Even by 1358 there were never more than three courts a year, and more often two or just the annual court with view of frankpledge; and since the entries are written continuously the abbey, with no involvement from the farmer, was holding both types.

The Manor's Roadside Verges

Because Hyde proper lacked ordinary residents and non-demesne lands it would seldom have featured in the court rolls. A booklet compiled in 1474 during the renewal of the warden of the new work's Knightsbridge rental, however, gives some extracts from the now-missing rolls, and includes the grant in 1466 to John Symonds of the piece of roadside wasteland on which he had recently built a leper house.[110] Since the house's site is well known and was on the northern verge immediately east of the bridge, this shows that waste adjoining Hyde had been placed under Knightsbridge. In 1483/4 the lazarcot was still the only tenement, and very probably the only grant from the waste, in this section of the warden's account.[111]

The legalism that in 1536 gifted part of Knightsbridge to Henry VIII because it was within the lease of Hyde may also have worked in the opposite direction, leaving the manorial waste verging Hyde with Knightsbridge rather than transferring it with the rest of Eye. Knightsbridge manor passed to the Crown in 1540 but was returned to the abbey's new dean and chapter in 1542, minus the large contribution to Hyde Park. This may explain how the northern roadside verge between the bridge and Hyde Park Corner became and remained part of Knightsbridge manor, but it is much less obvious why other pieces of land also were or were claimed to be so. The abbey's dean and chapter and, after the 1868 transfer, the Ecclesiastical Commissioners, issued a string of 18th- and 19th-century development leases for the southern roadside verge up to Hyde Park Corner, but perhaps the transfer of both the verges had seemed a simple practicality.[112]

The dean and chapter did, however, also hold some manorial waste land east of Park Lane.[113] Eye (apart from the parks) was sold on by the Crown, and at its eventual heiress' marriage in 1677 to Sir Thomas Grosvenor became part of the Grosvenor estate.[114] The estate suffered various diminutions through the standard practices of the Crown and the land market, but it has been claimed that the one that 'presents the most puzzling aspects is a plot with a frontage to Park Lane, about three acres in extent, immediately to the south of the Grosvenor estate, now occupied by the Dorchester Hotel and parts of Deanery and Tilney Streets. When first leased for building in the 1730s this was described as waste ground belonging to the manor of Knightsbridge in the ownership

108 WAM, 27009, 16446–9, 16335.
109 WAM, 16449 (1511).
110 WAM, 16335; for the leper house see below, 67–9.
111 WAM, 23559.
112 *Survey of London*, XLV, ch. 1.
113 See Roads, 7.
114 Gatty, *Mary Davies*, I, 222; *Survey of London*, XXXIX, 1–5.

Figure 10 *The art deco Dorchester Hotel, which opened in 1931.*

of the Dean and Chapter of Westminster.'[115] It was also termed 'a common or waste ... called Ossulton Common' in 18th-century Grosvenor estate documents.[116]

The dean and chapter's tenure of waste land on the east side of Park Lane can be taken back to at least 1665, when they let 2 a. 'in a place called Tybourne Lane' to Sir William Poultney.[117] Later leases show that the 2 a. consisted of two pieces, one abutting south on the 'High Road leading towards Hyde Park Corner' and east and north on Tyburn Lane, the other abutting west on the land, north on more dean and chapter waste, south on 'old tenements' belonging to Mr Davis and east 'in a Bevel Line on certain waste ground leading to Mayfair'.[118]

It is potentially far more puzzling that Sir Thomas Grosvenor was informed in 1682 that he had no claim on waste about to be inclosed in St James's Park as the king's law officers accepted the testimony of Sir William Poultney, who 'informeth Us, that the houses and Wast menconed in the said Petn have time out of mind belonged to the

---

115 *Survey of London*, XXXIX, 2, citing LMA, Middx Land Reg. 1738/4/11.

116 *Survey of London*, XXXIX, 2, citing Grosvenor Building Agreements, 75. Ossulston field had been lost to Hyde Park and Gatty's attempt at pinpointing Ossulston's location omits the field dimension: Gatty, *Mary Davies*, I, 54–9.

117 WAM, Reg. Bk XVII ff. 169v–170.

118 1721: WAM, Reg. Bk XXX ff. 143–5; for other detailed descriptions, WAM, 52634, *c.*1760 rehearsing 1718; WAM, 52262–3, n.d.

Deane and Chapter of Westminster and were never accounted any part of Ebury Farm'.[119] The abbey's comprehensive lease registers record Poultney as the lessee of two sets of waste, and of nothing else.[120] One of these was the 2 a. on Park Lane described above, the other, from 1665, three small tenements 'neere unto Hide Park' and a strip along the south side of the highway to Knightsbridge, all formerly let to William Benson.[121] The St James's Park extension produced the later Green Park whose north-western edge is at Hyde Park Corner, so this latter set might be relevant.[122] Poultney received new leases in 1674 and 1688, and in 1674 the description was unchanged.[123] In 1688, though, it became two houses 'or as much as stand on the waste of the manor of Knightsbridge' and the piece of ground ' lying all along from the turning of the corner of the new road leading between Westminster and Hyde Park toward the town of Knightsbridge'.[124] Even so this hardly seems to fit Sir William's testimony and perhaps, wittingly or not, he was mistaken.

Gatty noted in his history of the Grosvenor estate that James I's grant of Eybury specifically included its wasteland, and proffered the suggestion that the dean and chapter 'were granted the Manors of Knightsbridge and Westbourne Green in 1542, by Henry VIII, and these inclosures may have boiled over from the west side of the Westbourne to which they belong'.[125] Even this is an improvement on his initial draft sent to the Ecclesiastical Commissioners, which suggested that the dean and chapter had grabbed the land and then assumed squatters' rights. The commissioners were not amused and made some sensible general rebuttals, but could offer no specific alternative.[126]

The Formation of Hyde Park, Kensington Palace and Kensington Gardens

Hyde Park

In 1536 Henry VIII removed the whole of Eye including 'The site, soil, circuit and precinct of the Manor of Hyde, with all the demesne lands, rents, meadows and pastures of the said manor, with all other profits and commodities to the same pertaining or belonging, which be now in the tenure of one Thomas Arnold'.[127] Arnold briefly continued as before, except for paying his annual farm to the 'bailiff of the manors of la Nete, Eybury and Hyde', but by Michaelmas 1539 the whole of Hyde had gone into

119 Gatty, *Mary Davies*, I, 52–3.
120 WAM, card index to Reg. Bks.
121 WAM, Reg. Bk XVII ff. 153v–154.
122 Gatty, *Mary Davies*, I, 30 describes the park's extension and Poultney's compensation, but without connection to his comments at 52–3 about the waste.
123 WAM, Reg. Bk XX ff. 41–2.
124 WAM, Reg. Bk XXIII ff. 24–6; for later development, *Survey of London*, XLV, ch. 1.
125 Gatty, *Mary Davies*, I, 53.
126 WCA, Grosvenor Papers, Large Scrapbook no. 1.
127 *L&P Henry VIII*, vol. XI, no. 202; partly printed in Rutton, 'Eia', 57, who accidently puts *John* Arnold.

'the new park ... called le Hyde Park'.[128] This was before the abbey's final surrender on 16 January 1540, when all its remaining manors passed to the Crown; what was left of Knightsbridge was returned to the abbey's new dean and chapter in 1542.[129]

The demesnes of Hyde and Knightsbridge that formed the manor of Hyde provided the basis for the park but far from the whole of it. The park was an unbroken quadrilateral that at its first known measurement in 1652 covered 621.83 a. and reached roughly to today's Broad Walk.[130] This is substantially more than the 240 a. of the original 1358 lease of the joint demesnes.[131] In 1549 the parishioners of St Martin-in-the-Fields listed the commoning rights lost to 'All the Tenants of the Cytie of Westminster (which should mean St Margaret's) and the parishioners of Sent Martyns' and these included 'a farm called Hyde' containing 35 a. of meadow, 130 a. of arable and 80 a. of common 'being imparkyd wythe in thys xii yeres for the kyng'.[132] How exactly this worked is unclear – the leases had never referred to a separate common, and land outside the farm was also lost for lammas commoning, but that the total of 245 a. is so close to the 1358 figure and so far from the total for Hyde Park is certainly interesting.

The demesnes, as we have seen, were never a solid block. The 1478 description shows that the open fields were largely inclosed, so some strip swapping and consolidation had probably occurred, but closes on both sides of the river still had non-demesne abuttals, and those on the east were partly bounded by Stonehill and Mabelcroft rather than extending to Park Lane.[133] Mabelcroft features regularly in earlier records, for instance in the de Kendales' 1291 acquisition of 5 a. '*iuxta* la Hyde' lying between some of their lands 'towards Mabilecroft', but there is no sign that it was ever transferred from Eybury to Hyde.[134] Stonehill is among the few easily traced additions to the park because the farmer of Eybury's resultant rent loss was repeatedly logged in the royal records.[135] The transfers of Stonehill (40 a.) and Tiborne Close (15 a., probably inclosed since 1478 from Mabelcroft) have been misinterpreted because while Hyde was seen as a solid block bounded by Park Lane any inclusion from Eybury seemed to imply shifting the road.[136] The Eybury farmer also suffered other less well known losses to the park: 2 a. recently purchased from Nicholas Goodyer and the rent from 7 a. of the St James's Hospital lands. The hospital's estate was acquired in 1531 primarily to create St James's Park but it included an outlying 18 a. 'at Knightsbridge'.[137]

The 1520 lease of the 'site of Knightsbridge manor' must have been terminated alongside other compulsory purchases, but the process is largely hidden.[138] A 1568 report into 1 a. of pasture in St Margaret's parish lying between the park to the north and king's highway to the south stated that it had been bought among other land by Henry VIII 'to

128 TNA, SC 6/Hen VIII/2101–3.
129 See above, 14.
130 Rutton, 'Kensington Gardens', 145.
131 WAM, 16265, also Reg. Bk II ff. 154v–155.
132 McMaster, *St Martin*, 254–5.
133 WAM, 4870, see Appendix, 79.
134 WAM, 4874.
135 E.g. TNA, SC 6/EdwVI/298.
136 Davis, 'Conduit'; Gatty, *Mary Davies*, I, 32–3; see also above, 7.
137 See below, 68.
138 WAM, 16286, Reg. Bk II ff. 154v–155.

be inclosed into Hyde Park. And for that it would have bought the pale out of square the king's pleasure was it should be left out of the said park'.[139] The guider of Knightsbridge leper hospital claimed in 1595 that his hospital's solitary piece of landed endowment had been lost to the park, and although there cannot have been any major removal it is possible that the site was trimmed to achieve the pale's 'square'.[140]

In 1569 a park keeper was ordered to rail in some 40 a. of 'our (i.e. the queen's) land called Knightsbridge land' as a deer inclosure from which horses and cattle were to be entirely debarred, but since the rest of Knightsbridge was not the queen's this must have been an internal rearrangement.[141] Because the park area was removed from local control it barely features in the later Knightsbridge court rolls other than as a boundary to developments on the roadside waste. In a rare exception the manor jury reported in 1586 that the queen's park was 'extremely ruined and in great decay' and humbly requested repair, but dramatic as this sounds it will only have referred to the perimeter fencing.[142] Similarly in 1618 Henry Rich, the park keeper, was reported for failing to scour 'le Parke Ditch' between Knightsbridge and Gore.[143]

Rich's responsibility stopped at the park's south-west corner, opposite Gore and, on this side of the road, some way east of the boundary with Kensington. Such restraint seems so uncharacteristic of Henry VIII that it is obvious to wonder if the intervening land had been disparked for a royal favourite, but this cannot have been the case since descriptions compiled in 1616 and 1619 show a landscape of closes and fields whose names are those of the pre-park era.[144] Comparing them with the 1478 description and the court rolls does however suggest that the demesnes too had stopped short of the border – Isabella Arnolde was repeatedly in 1515–24 told to mend her close lying between 'the demesne lands of the manor of Hyde and the common field of Knightsbridge'.[145] It seems very likely that although the king had to fill all the gaps in his rectangle he decided not to enlarge it beyond the demesne edge.

Kensington Palace and Kensington Gardens

It was the house built *c.*1618 for Sir George Coppin in the strip of land between Hyde Park and the Kensington boundary that was sold to William III in 1689. It was rebuilt and became Kensington Palace, and most of the western side of Hyde Park was added to its own grounds to form Kensington Gardens, thus successfully completing Knightsbridge's occlusion. The history of the pre-palace house (but not of the later palace) is therefore central to this book's themes, and to show that it was firmly in Knightsbridge/Westminster is to correct almost all the previous historiography.[146]

---

139 WAM, 16274; *Survey of London*, XLV, 43.

140 WAM, 16311; the Spittle Meads were too far south and had in any case belonged to St James's Hospital: see below, 68.

141 Davis, *Knightsbridge*, 19–20.

142 WAM, 16452, m. 12: *valde ruinosum et in magno decasu*. For comparable descriptions of the abbey's park see below, 48.

143 WAM, 16453, m. 14; On Rich as keeper, see below, 36 n. 147.

144 TNA, C 54 230/7, C 54 2417/11; see Appendix, 80–1.

145 WAM, 16449, 4870; see Appendix, 77–80.

146 For the official Kensington Palace account published in 2003, see above, 3.

If the house had remained in private hands the Kensington link would never have been firmly asserted but once Kensington Palace was in existence earlier justifying links were assumed and claimed. There turns out to be no support for these in any of the pre-palace records. Because the house was in a belt of land isolated on the east by Hyde Park its inhabitants naturally turned towards Kensington, the house became Kensington House, and lawyers became uncertain enough to hedge their bets, but inhabitants and administrators were normally well aware that there was no actual connection.

The Estate under Sir Walter Cope, Sir Henry Rich and Sir George Coppin

Even historians who know where the Kensington boundary lay have still assumed a link, usually because the land involved at one stage belonged to Walter Cope (c.1553–1614, knighted 1603), who became lord of the manor of Abbots Kensington in 1599. He also built and lived in 'Cope Castle', renamed Holland House in 1624 when Sir Henry Rich (1590–1649), husband of Cope's heiress daughter, became 1st earl of Holland. Among many profitable offices Cope also managed to become joint- and then sole keeper of Hyde Park from 1610 until his death, when the role passed to Rich.[147] But to think that Cope's possession of the land (or, more probably, most of it) meant that it became attached to Kensington is to misunderstand the nature of the land market, where cross-border accumulations such as his were a regular occurrence. Cope's acquisitions were part of a wave of elite expansion westward, with various members of an interconnected circle of lawyers, courtiers and parliamentarians moving out from more central addresses. These included Cope, Rich, Sir George Coppin and Sir Heneage Finch (the next two purchasers of the pre-palace estate), Sir Baptist Hicks of Campden Hill, just across the Kensington border, and Sir William Blake on a cross-border estate in Brompton and Knightsbridge.[148] Because all these accumulations were tied to the wealth of their owners, dispersal was as normal as accumulation.[149]

In turning to the detail of the pre-palace estate, the mutability is there from the earliest known reference, in a Knightsbridge rental of 1597/8 which lists 'Mr Cope' and Samuell Hassellwood as holding parts of 'Mustians free land'.[150] If, as seems likely, this was part of the eventual house site, Cope must have done some subsequent buying out. Mustian and Muschamp are apparently forms of the same name and the family was active on both sides of the border; it was William Muschamp of Kensington who in 1568 acquired the lease of the acre saved from the park and both he and other family members reappear below.[151] Cope was also reported in January 1598 for making an 8-a. close called Halfhyde; Halfhyde had once been much larger but was mostly lost to the park.[152]

---

147   Faulkner, *Kensington*, 413, citing MS Cal. Pat. 10 James I, 23 no. 17, a reference overlooked in *Hist. Parl. Commons* 1604–29, VI, 30, which says Rich was keeper 'by 1630'.
148   *Hist. Parl. Commons* 1604–29: Cope III, 658–62, Rich VI, 30–2, Finch IV, 257–69, Hicks IV, 690–3; for Coppin, Merritt, *W (2)*, passim; for Blake, Settlement and Development, 57–8; his neighbour Sir Robert Fenn, although part of the same milieu, acquired his estate by inheritance: Settlement and Development, 61–3.
149   Cf the dispersal of the Blake and Moreau estates, Settlement and Development, 58–9.
150   WAM, 40627.
151   WAM, 16274. I owe the Mustian/Muschamp suggestion to Olivia Fryman.
152   WAM, 16453 m. 9.

Cope's will (1614) shows him drowning in debt.[153] Rich as heir was by far the leading executor but various others, including Cope's 'loving friend' Coppin, remained involved. Much of Cope's accumulated property had to be sold and Coppin bought almost all the land between Hyde Park and the Kensington boundary. First, in July 1616 for £260, Rich sold him 11½ a. of pasture in St Margaret's parish bounded east by Hyde Park, south by Agmundesham Muschampe's land in Crane Field and Rich's lands, and west and north by more of Rich's lands.[154] Then in July 1619 Coppin paid £1,200 for all of Rich's adjacent lands, and a detailed title deed helpfully summarises the location: between the London to Acton road north and London to Brentford road south, 'Hide Parke pale', Coppin's previous purchase and Crane Field east, and the gravel pits, vicarage land, Cunduite Close and land late of William Muschampe deceased west.[155]

The 1619 lands seem to have been attached to three tenanted buildings. Two of these, the White Hart occupied by Robert Prudam and a neighbouring house occupied by John Stoning, were firmly in St Margaret's parish and on the London to Brentford Road.[156] The third was 'in some or one' of the parishes of Kensington, St Margaret's and Paddington and had lately been divided; its previous tenant and one of the current ones also held the gravel pits which lay immediately west of the sale. Excluding the unmeasured buildings and their immediate grounds, the second transfer came to 43½ a. 1 r., thus providing a grand total of 55 a. 1 r. Of the three named parishes only Kensington had no unequivocal assignments and most if not all the equivocal ones, most obviously 4 a. near Hyde Park pale, were clearly unjustified. Although accumulated estates could easily cross manor and parish boundaries, as both Cope's and Coppin's did, this particular cluster stayed notably east of the Kensington boundary. Perhaps most of the lands to the immediate west had already been bound into the vicarage/Campden estate.[157]

The two definitive documents of 1616 and 1619 have only recently come to light and some of Faulkner's confusion in his still-indispensable *History of Kensington* (1820) was because he was working from more opaque sources. It has now also become clear that Coppin remained caught up in Rich's problems and himself died in debt, and it is this complicated background of interrelated debts that explains why the transfers were not straightforward. Coppin died in February or March 1620 and in April 1621 his widow Anne and eldest son Robert (a minor) entered a complaint in Chancery concerning the nearby land of Notting Wood, immediately north of the Bayswater Road in Kensington.[158] Rich had transferred this in June 1616 to Coppin and two others to sell to settle debts for which they were guarantors, but when other potential purchasers withdrew Coppin was reluctantly persuaded to buy. The transfer happened in January 1620 but for all his widow's protestations the debts had probably not been settled.

---

153 TNA, PROB 11/125/121; *Hist. Parl. Commons* 1604–29, III, 658–62, VI, 30–2.

154 TNA, C 54 230/7; see Appendix, 80. I am very grateful to Olivia Fryman for directing me towards both these documents.

155 TNA, C 54 2417/11; Appendix, 80–1.

156 For the roadside location see below, 43.

157 See *Survey of London*, XXXVII and Fryman, *Kensington Palace*.

158 TNA, C 3/305/13. I am grateful to Olivia Fryman for the reference and for discussion. TNA, C 4/341/86 confirms that Coppin died in debt.

Because Coppin's heir was a minor a jury was empanelled to state his inheritance and reported in May 1620. It described the lands in Kensington, Paddington and Westbourne of which Sir George had died seized, including Notting Wood (120½ a.), and then continued that he ought also to have been seized of the three tenements and lands he had bought in 1616 and 1619 but that these were still being held by Rich.[159] Meanwhile a separate inquest in April 1620 produced a seizure in July of some of Cope's (i.e. Rich's) estate to satisfy a debt to Nicholas Salter. Under the heading 'Certain lands and tenements in Kensington and Westminster' are four farms: (1) The manors of Earls Court and Abbots Kensington in Kensington (2) Also in Kensington, 80 a. of wood called Nottingwood and 30 a. in Clay Field (3) A messuage in Westminster called the White Hart (4) A messuage in Kensington called the west town.[160] Rich soon regained the manors so the seizure was probably temporary, but the Coppin claim to the White Hart was being disregarded.

Neither of these inquests matches well with Sir George's will, written on 19 February and proved on 6 March 1620. He gave only a summary description, bequeathing his wife his 'nowe dwellinge house' in St Martin-in-the-Fields and one 'late builte' in St Margaret's, 'with all my Lands within the sayd parish of St Margarettes nowe in the tenure or occupacion of one [blank] Prudam Innkeeper. And all my Landes and tenements commonly called Nottingwood and all other landes tenements and hereditaments in Middlesex'.[161] He therefore thought he was holding the new house and the White Hart and its lands (where Prudam was named as tenant in the 1619 transfer), as well as Notting Wood. The house and the White Hart were part of the Knightsbridge estate in 1662.[162]

The May 1620 jurors mentioned the house in St Martin-in-the-Fields but not the new one in St Margaret's, yet Sir George must surely have had possession of its site to have started building. He is listed in the Knightsbridge court rolls in 1618 as one of five freeholders in default of suit and first appears in the Knightsbridge part of the St Margaret's overseers' accounts for the April to April accounting year 1618/9, both references ahead of his more major purchase of July 1619.[163] This strongly suggests that the house had just been built on the land bought in July 1616 and it cannot, of course, have predated that purchase. Unfortunately two influential authorities on the house and its presumed architect, John Thorpe, were unaware that Coppin had previously owned the forerunner of Sheffield House, just across the Kensington border, which he had brought from Cope in 1603 but sold by 1613.[164] They therefore conflated the two, and in asserting that Thorpe's house was on land in Kensington bought from Cope in

159 TNA, WARD 7/61/222. The total acreage for the 1619 lands is given at only 36½ a. 1 r. but some of the contributory figures (though not the actual lands) are missing.

160 Paper in bundle TNA, E 192/16/3; for the seizure warrant see also TNA, SP 46/70 f. 194. The May 1620 jurors gave Coppin at least 22 a. in Clay Field.

161 TNA, PROB 11/135/275, repeated within TNA, WARD 7/61/222.

162 Not to be confused with the White Hart on the leper hospital site.

163 WAM, 16453 m. 14; WCA, E150, film 2351. I am grateful to Olivia Fryman for the latter reference and discussion.

164 TNA, C 54/1791; *Survey of London*, XXXVII, 42, wrongly suggests Coppin moved straight from Kensington to the new Knightsbridge house.

1603 obviously supported the supposed Kensington link.[165] Some of their chronology
of the evolution of Thorpe's designs is also based on this mistake. Coppin described
his Knightsbridge house as 'late builte' in February 1620 but never moved there and
his widow and children only did so in 1622.[166] Summerson suggested that the house
was unfinished until then but resolution of the debt issue seems another possibility.[167]
Lady Anne appears in the St Margaret's overseers' accounts until 1624/5 but by 1625/6
the occupier was Sir Heneage Finch (1580–1631), and the rest of the house's pre-palace
history is with the Finches.[168]

The Estate under the Finches, 1625/6–1689

Sir Heneage's first wife died in 1627 leaving him with four young children, and he
married a rich widow, Elizabeth Bennett, in 1629.[169] His luck was little better than
Coppin's and in his own will, made on 16 April and proved on 7 December 1631, he
bequeathed Elizabeth a life interest in 'my dwellinge house neere Kensington with
the gardens and grounds thereto adioyninge [and] all other the landes I lately bought
of Mr Muschampe or Mr Coppin'.[170] (Lady Anne Coppin in fact had the life interest
in all her husband's Middlesex properties and was put ahead of her sons in sale
documents.) Sir Heneage had therefore already enlarged Coppin's estate, although by
how much is unclear. In 1638 Agmundishawe Muschampe, who had held the only
non-Rich abuttal to Coppin's 1616 purchase, settled with the abbey's dean and chapter
for 39-years' quitrent owed for free land in Knightsbridge.[171] On the other hand Finch
did not purchase Coppin's nearby Kensington lands, including Notting Wood, which
descended to Coppin's heirs.[172]

Heneage also stated that after Elizabeth's death the house should be sold unless
his 'dear brother Francis' wanted it, in which case to him for life and then the sale. He
carefully placed the house 'neere Kensington' but bequeathed £3 to its parish poor
and 10s. apiece to 'to the twelve poore women at Kensington to whom I have for some
tyme given some small weekly reliefe'.[173] The re-widowed Elizabeth was left with her
own son, three young stepsons, Heneage, Francis and John, a stepdaughter, one joint
daughter and another on the way.[174] In the event she and her brother-in-law Francis
(himself a widower since 1621) both made the house their home, receiving certificates

165 P.A. Faulkner, 'Nottingham House. John Thorpe and his relation to Kensington Palace', *Archaeol. Jnl*, 107
(1950), 66–77; having noted that Coppin was buried in the church of St Martin-in-the-Fields, Faulkner
adds, bizarrely, 'in which Parish the Kensington house lay'; J. Summerson (ed.), *The Book of Architecture
of John Thorpe in Sir John Soane's Museum*, Walpole Soc. 40 (1966), 6, 36, 71, plan T 94.

166 Dame Anne and Robert, both of St Margaret's parish, leased the St Martin's house to Endymion Porter
on 3 June 1622: LMA, BRA723/8.

167 Summerson, *Book of Architecture of John Thorpe*, 71.

168 WCA, E151, microfilm 2352. I am grateful to Olivia Fryman for the reference, which corrects the *Hist.
Parl. Commons 1604–29*, IV, 267 association of the purchase with Bennett money.

169 *Conway Letters*, 2.

170 TNA, PROB 11/160/764.

171 TNA, C 54/2320/7; WAM, 16453 m. 16; his debt also features at m. 14 (1618) and in WAM, 41390 (1610).

172 Faulkner, *Kensington*, 430.

173 TNA, PROB 11/160/764.

174 *Conway Letters*, 2.

of residence in 1641 under the double heading, 'Within the Liberties Westminster St Margarettes' and, below that, Kensington.[175] In 1642 the Kensington parish registers, in the first of many relevant entries, record the burial of a 'servant to the Lady Finch, of the parish of St Margretts, Westminster'.[176] Anne, Sir Heneage's posthumous daughter, married Edward Conway at Kensington in 1651 and during the next decade whenever she was living with her mother the correspondence address was always 'at Kensington'.[177]

Lady Conway's letters confirm that her uncle was also normally there. Uncertainty about the ownership is perhaps reflected in the first known description of Hyde Park, made when it was put up for sale in six divisions during the Interregnum in 1652; the south-western, Kensington Division was bounded on the west by 'part of the house and ground usually taken to belong to Mr Finch of Kensington' while above it Gravel Pit Division was bounded by 'the ground lying near the Gravel Pits, and part of Finch's ground'.[178]

Francis died at the turn of 1657/8 having 'settled his estate by deed', and his nuncupative will only notes the change of executor from Heneage to his stepmother.[179] Elizabeth's own will was made in July 1657 and proved in February 1662.[180] She does not mention her life interests and provides no detail on the residual estate bequeathed to her Finch daughters and some lands in Kensington bought of Mr Mustian and bequeathed to a cousin. But in a codicil added in August 1660 she decreed that 'The landes by mee purchased lying in the Feild where the Marble Conduit stands, and uppon which some parte of the said Marble Conduit may be thought to be built or some part of the Grove adioyneing may be thought to growe I doe give to my sonne in lawe [ie stepson] Sir Heneage Finch and his heires for the prevention of all suites in law between him and those who shall clayme under mee'. The prospect of lawsuits is obviously interesting, and so too is the land's location. Cunduite Close was immediately west of Coppin's 1619 purchase and was in Kensington. The *Survey of London* traces the descent but, unaware of Elizabeth's purchase, says only that by 1672 slightly over half of its 4 a. had passed into Sir Heneage's ownership; after this part passed to the Crown it became the forcing ground and then the barracks site.[181] It was contiguous with the palace grounds but remained a clear cross-border extrusion.

Elizabeth's codicil implies that Heneage junior was to inherit the family home, but Heneage senior had willed that it be sold after Elizabeth and Francis senior's death. This

175 TNA, E 115/151/81; E 115/152/132; For Francis see below and *Hist. Parl. Commons* 1604–29, IV, 256–7, although it misses this dimension and gives his residences only as Inner Temple and, through his wife, Bromley, Middx.

176 F.N. Macnamara and A. Storey-Maskelyne (eds), *The Parish Register of Kensington, co. Middlesex from AD 1539–AD 1675* (London 1890), 117, 73; Faulkner, *Kensington*, 257–68, uninterested in servants, missed this.

177 *Par. Reg. of Kensington*, 73; *Conway Letters*, passim.

178 Rutton, 'Kensington Gardens', 145–9; Faulkner, *Kensington*, 413–15. Gender bias is also possible.

179 TNA, PROB 11/272/252, from a register that can only be viewed online: http://discovery.nationalarchives. gov.uk/details/r/C12122 (accessed 18 Mar. 2016), provides no actual will. A summary in *Abstract of Wills PCC Wootton 1658*, I, no. 78, says Elizabeth was the sole beneficiary, as does *Hist. Parl. Commons* 1604–29, IV, 256–7, but this may be a misreading.

180 TNA, PROB 11/307/365.

181 *Survey of London*, XXXVII, 29, 192.

perhaps required some legal footwork or at least an agreement to buy out the inheritor's brothers. Although Elizabeth's will was not proved until February 1662 she had died by October 1661.[182] Faulkner, citing a document 'communicated by Mr Palmer', said that in 1661 Heneage junior purchased the house from his younger brother John, who also 'covenants against incumbrances etc committed by his brother Francis'.[183] Palmer's document said Hilary Term 14 Charles II, which is almost certainly early 1662, and a later version of the transaction enrolled on 3 June specifically superseded a fine levied early that year in the Court of Common Pleas.[184]

John Finch and Sir Edward Dering transferred the estate to Heneage. John received £2,500 and Dering, whose role was notional, 5s. Dering (whose wife and Heneage's were sisters) was also the plaintiff in the fine in Common Pleas against John and Heneage.[185] The transfer certainly covered the whole estate, specifying among other things the capital messuage 'neere Kensington in the parish of Westminster' with 'all the hanginges furniture and other the moveables in the said capitall messauge now beinge', all its lands abutting east on the pale of Hyde Park and north and south on the main roads, plus the close by the marble conduit, the White Hart and several other demised (leased out) properties. Since Elizabeth had purchased the close and willed it to Heneage, John and Francis's involvement cannot have been as Faulkner envisaged, and John's warranty against Francis's incumbrances was probably simply the survivor acting to cover both. Francis remains a shadowy figure but seems, like the uncle with whom he is easily confused, to have died in the later 1650s.[186] It would be interesting to know which of them was the author of the *Discourse* and Orinda's Palaemon.[187]

The transfer is mostly couched in terms of the whole estate but at one point it says more accurately 'of and in one moiety', and this moiety (part, usually a half), whatever its rationale, had never amounted to actual possession. The 'Mr Finch' cited in the 1652 description of Hyde Park must have been Francis senior, who on the verge of death in 1657/8 made Elizabeth his executor having previously 'settled his estate by deed'. Confusion over their relative roles might explain the Knightsbridge court roll for 4 May 1661, which opens with a list of those in default of suit headed by Lady Elizabeth and then immediately states that Francis Finch who held in free tenure a messuage with appurtenances in the manor, had died since the last court.[188] Elizabeth had died by October 1661 and although Heneage was the named executor it seems from the Conway letters that by April 1662 it was John and his two half-sisters who were dealing with the administration.[189] In March, though, Heneage was granted the ditch or fence that

182 TNA, PROB 11/307/365; *Conway Letters*, 196, 201.

183 Faulkner, *Kensington*, 329–30.

184 Palmer's letter is doc. 16 in the illustrated Faulkner, BL, L.R. 271 c.3; Hil. Term started a week after 20 Jan. and the regnal year 14 Charles II on 30 Jan.: C.R. Cheney, *A Handbook of Dates* (revised edn, 2000), 98, 40. TNA, C 54/4097/33.

185 For the relationship see *Conway Letters*, 201, 206.

186 Faulkner, *Kensington* 331. Francis junior appears unambiguously in the *Conway Letters* between 20 Oct. 1651 and 1 May 1657 and in none of the slightly later family wills. A different Francis Finch, *c.*1602–77, was active in the 1660s as an MP and collector of excise, cf *Hist. Parl. Commons* 1660–90, II, 315–17.

187 W.G. Hiscock, 'Friendship, Francis Finch's Discourse and the Circle of the Matchless Orinda', *The Rev. of Eng. Studies*, XV no. 60 (Oct. 1939), 466–8; *Hist. Parl. Commons* 1604–29, IV, 256–7.

188 WAM, 16454 m. 1; this is the first court record since 23 Mar. 1632, WAM, 16453 m. 15.

189 *Conway Letters*, 196, 201; TNA, PROB 11/307/365.

Figure 11 *The funerary monument to Sir John Finch (1626–82) and his partner Sir Thomas Baines (1622–80) in Christ's College, Cambridge.*

separated his land from Hyde Park plus a ten-foot wide strip, a remarkable transfer by Charles II.[190]

The house was substantial – assessed at 26 hearths in 1664.[191] Within Kensington, though, the Finches remained very minor landowners, something that Faulkner, in quoting two 1670s documents, demonstrated without recognising the significance. In 1672 the Kensington manor jurors stated that the manor boundaries extended eastward with those of the parish up to 'the lands belonging to the manor of Paddington, and the manor of Westminster' – so no cross-border claim.[192] Then in 1675 they furnished a list

190 *Cal. SP Dom.* 1661–2, 297, 320.
191 TNA, LMA/MR/TH7 f. 24 via http://www.hearthtax.org.uk (accessed 15 Dec. 2015).
192 Faulkner, *Kensington*, 428.

of the major freeholders, who ranged from Sir Richard Anderson with 400 a. through the earl of Warwick & Holland (Rich's descendent) 204 a., Mr Coppin (Sir George's descendent) 196 a., Viscount Campden 90 a., Mr Halsey 20 a., Vicarage glebe 13 a., down to Heneage, Lord Finch, with 9 a.[193] Faulkner also added, wrongly but symptomatically, that the Coppin lands became part of Kensington Gardens. Heneage became 1st earl of Nottingham in 1681 and in 1689 his son and heir Daniel sold Kensington House to William III for £20,000.[194]

The evolution of Kensington Palace and Kensington Gardens are amply covered elsewhere but a few concluding points are worth making.[195] First, in the absence of a transfer deed and perhaps because contemporary accounts focus on William's new house and its small but attractive garden, it has sometimes been thought that the king bought only the house and immediate ground to the south.[196] But the new detail on the Coppin-Finch lands, and indeed common sense, suggest that the order to treat with Nottingham 'about his house and estate' envisaged a general transfer. The comment in 1691 that 'they were digging up a flat of 4 a. or 5 a. to enlarge their garden' merely indicates enlargement across what had previously been kept as fields or park.[197] The 1616–19 purchases came to just over 55 a. excluding the unmeasured White Hart and other demised properties, and Conduit Close probably added another 4 a. Charles II's grant contributed a little more and that Heneage had 9 a. in Kensington by 1675 suggests other small additions.[198]

There is, however, uncertainty around the properties listed as demised in 1662. These comprised the White Hart, 'all the other messuages thereunto adioyning and newly erected' and the White Hart's accompanying lands, all let to Robert Harewood, butcher; another 'messuage or tenement' with appurtenances 'in or neere Kensington'; and unspecified 'lands and tenements' let to others.[199] In September 1690 the Crown purchased a strip of land 200 ft long and 31 inches wide immediately west of the way leading from 'the common road from Kensington to London to their Majesties' new palace of Kensington'. The strip was to be laid into the way and separated by a brick wall from the garden of the White Hart, a messuage in the possession of the strip's seller, Matthew Child.[200] That Child was able to sell and also undertake some restrictive covenants suggests he was the freeholder. There is no sign of any later Crown possession of the road-fronting block immediately west of Palace Avenue and below Palace Green.[201] Various maps show buildings with rear gardens and including, in 1871, a pub next to Palace Avenue, but by 1894 the site had been redeveloped for the Royal Palace Hotel, predecessor to today's Royal Garden Hotel.[202] The Crown's need to purchase the strip in 1690 (for £400), perhaps suggests the White Hart and adjoining properties had been sold

193 Ibid., 430.
194 With thanks to Olivia Fryman: *Cal. Treasury Bks*, IX (1688–92): 11 Jun. (order to treat with Nottingham), 37, and 19 Jul. (payment of first instalment), 42; for the 2nd and 1st earls see *Hist. Parl. Commons* 1660–90, II, 312–15, 317–22; the family tree at 313 is very limited.
195 Fryman, *Kensington Palace*; Rutton, 'Kensington Gardens', 149–50; LUCKG; LUCHP.
196 LUCKG, 20, states that the garden covered 17½ a.
197 Rutton, 'Kensington Gardens', 149–50, also thought the whole estate was purchased.
198 Faulkner, *Kensington*, 428.
199 TNA, C 54/4097/33.
200 *Cal. Treasury Bks*, IX (1688–92), 808.
201 *Survey of London*, XXXVII, chs 8–9.
202 See Frontispiece, iv–v; Map 3, above, 19; Map 6, below, 44; *Old OS Maps*, London 74 (1871, 1894).

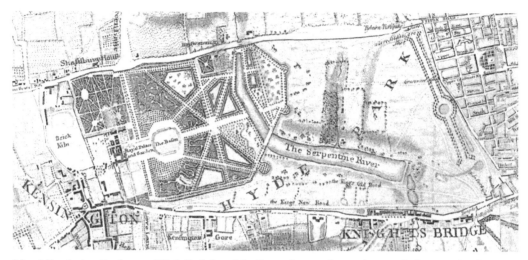

Map 6 *Kensington Gardens and Hyde Park from John Rocque's map of 1746, showing the bastioned wall.*

before 1689. If the other tenements demised in 1662 were located elsewhere on the estate, the leases must at some point have been terminated and the buildings destroyed.

Conversion into a royal residence had several immediate effects. Hyde Park, still very much an area of elite display, now faced west as much as east, a shift encouraged by William's construction of Rotten Row to connect his new palace across the park to Westminster.[203] William's decision to name his new residence Kensington Palace not only gave royal authority to a Kensington link but also, from a Kensington perspective, greatly increased the link's desirability. Knightsbridge's occlusion was already well underway, thanks to Hyde Park, but if the Finch estate had remained in private hands the Kensington link would not have been so strongly pursued, Kensington Gardens would not have been created and the 1900 boundary change would not have occurred.

After the royal purchase the main topographical changes happened in the first three decades of the 18th century, when most of the western side of Hyde Park was transferred into the new (and newly landscaped) Kensington Gardens and the Westbourne transformed into the Long Water (1727) and Serpentine (1731).[204] It is easy today to assume that at this stage the river acquired yet another boundary function, separating Kensington Gardens from Hyde Park, but this was not entirely the case. Kensington Gardens, defined by a wall built in 1730, included Buck Hill on the north-east side of the river, and a strip of Hyde Park continued south of the wall to bring the slightly diverted Rotten Row and the King's New Road, (South Carriage Drive, 1735/6) across to the palace. This is why the sites for the 1851 Great Exhibition and the Albert Memorial (1872), although west of the river, were taken from Hyde Park. The wall west of the river was demolished in 1868 and in 1870 this southern strip of Hyde Park was transferred to Kensington Gardens. East of the river the wall went in 1916; doing so and filling in the ha ha would, it was hoped, remove an opportunity for 'immorality'.[205]

---

203 LUCHP, 11. Rotten Row is marked on Map 6 as the King's Old Road.
204 For the whole of this paragraph, and comprehensive detail, Rutton, 'Kensington Gardens', LUCHP and LUCKG.
205 LUCHP, 20, n. 59.

ECONOMIC HISTORY

Agriculture

COURT ROLLS, ACCOUNTS AND deeds present a fairly standard picture but one particularly worth excavating because so much was destroyed by the parks. The arable 'fields of Knightsbridge' were Northfield and Southfield, separated by the main road, and the fields east of the river which contributed to Hyde were, as shown above, Cresswell and Ossulston. All were initially open fields divided into shots or furlongs (*culturae*) and within the shots into strips.

There was never any general inclosure, but between the 15th and early 17th centuries the area conformed to the pattern around London in gradually abandoning arable and moving to pasture crofts and closes. The transformation of Northfield is visible in the descriptions of 1478, 1616 and 1619.[1] Some of the closes received new names but others preserved ones previously encountered in the sowing accounts of 1357/8.[2] In the earlier records duplication of descriptive names sometimes makes a location uncertain: in particular there were two Horseleys, one near the site of Knightsbridge manor and the other in Southfield; La Dune, or Down, appears in records of Eye and Knightsbridge; and scribes sometimes failed to distinguish between Westbourne's Southlond and Knightsbridge's Southfield. No potentially ambiguous references are cited here.

Although Northfield was fully transferred to pasture, a large part of Southfield became part of the Brompton Park Nursery in the 1680s, and throughout Knightsbridge the overlaying gravels ensured a fair degree of fertility. Surpluses beyond the requirements of the abbey and local *familia* (demesne household) were regularly sold, and in 1293/4, for example, the *serviens* (whose accounts always included Westbourne) made £6 6s. 10d. from the sale of 8 quarters of wheat, 5 of barley, 4 of oats, 3 of dredge (a mix of barley and oats) and 1 of peas, as well as 3s. 4d. from honey.[3] In 1335/6, again for example, he sowed 37½ a. of wheat, 20½ a. of maslin (a mix of wheat and rye), 30 a. of barley, 42 a. of oats, 3¼ a. of dredge, 5¾ a. of beans and 4¾ a. of peas within various shots; most of these can be identified and they were overwhelmingly on the gravels below the Bayswater Road.[4] By 1353/4, when Hyde was being directly managed with Knightsbridge manor, the pattern was similar although Hyde provided mainly maslin, rye and dredge; by now too some demesne land was at farm: a 20-a. field called Halfhyde

1   WAM, 4870, TNA, C 54 230/7, C 54 2417/11; see Appendix, 77–81.
2   WAM, 16443; names included Brokeshot, Daubereshot, Kassewellshot (i.e. Cresswellshot), Welleplot.
3   WAM, 16384.
4   WAM, 16420.

Figure 12 *The central garden in Montpelier Square is now the largest piece of unbuilt land from the former Southfield. The development was laid out in the mid 1820s but took 30 years to complete.*

(on the Knightsbridge–Westbourne border), Squabbeslond (in Southfield), 12 a. of 'land, meadow and pasture' in Kerswelle (i.e. Cresswell), and 36 a. in Westbourne.[5]

Long before the general transfer to pasture, animals were probably as important as arable to Knightsbridge's demesne economy. Considerable profits were generated from demesne livestock and, to a lesser but locally vital extent, from selling access to pasturing. In 1293/4 when the *serviens* made £6 6*s.* 10*d.* from selling surplus crops, he also made £6 6*s.* 4*d.* from selling old and dead animals and another £1 12*s.* 3*d.* from milk, some 200 cheeses, butter, pasturage and straw.[6] The dairying probably owed more to the significant amount of meadow produced by the river, springs and consequent drainage ditches than to poor soil. The Hyde manor house was moated, and this was presumably the ditch 'next to the court of John de la Hyde' from which the Eybury reeve sold the pasture in 1281.[7] New closes were routinely bounded by ditches and the court rolls are full of orders to keep them scoured. In 1408–9, for example, the demesne farmer was told to scour three ditches (*fossat'*), repair the drain (*gurges*) that was flooding the main road to Kensington and cease diverting the watercourse next to Southfield.[8]

5   WAM, 16438.
6   WAM, 16384.
7   WAM, 26855.
8   WAM, 16447 mm. 5–6.

Like the arable, the demesne meadows seem all to have been south of the Bayswater Road, and a supplementary meadow in Chelsea was also often rented. In 1301/2, for example, the *serviens* accounted for the sale of grazing from two ditches in le Halvehyde and the costs of haymaking in Horsmede, Lutletaddecroft, the meadow of La More, and next to the Thames.[9] In 1328/9 12 cows, 1 bullock and grazing for 100 sheep were farmed out and 10*d.* from pasture at le Hoke was correspondingly absent; 8*d.* was received for pasture at le Southfield but nothing from Halvehid and Tadecroft because they were fallow.[10] In 1478 the demesnes east of the river in Hyde included Long Meadow and Galowmede, and the site of Hyde manor included a range of livestock-related buildings.[11]

Most of the enduring woodland was beyond the gravel on the bare clay of Westbourne (and also Paddington), but limited areas survived further south. Faggots (bundles of twigs) were regularly sold from Estgrove, to whose wood and underwood demesne farmers were granted only limited rights.[12] This was probably identical with the Grove of Knightsbridge in which pasture was farmed (let) in the early 15th century; the 1520 grant of the site of Knightsbridge manor included permission to grub up wood.[13] When Hidegrove was farmed with Hyde the farm still excluded all wood and underwood.[14] Large areas of common, which normally co-existed with extensive demesne woodland, seem to be absent here, despite the St Martin's parishioners' claim in 1549 that emparking the 'farm called Hyde' had removed 35 a. of meadow, 130 a. of arable and 80 a. of common.[15] The first reference to Knightsbridge Green, at the junction of the main and Brompton Roads, comes in 1474 when a messuage on 'le grene apud Knyghtbrigge' was let along with the site of the manor.[16] In 1693 land there was described as part of the 'Common or wast ground', but even before subsequent inclosure this was a small area, and may simply have been the generous waste of a road junction.[17]

All the references to commoning are to lammas rights, pasturage across the fields between Lammas Day and Candlemas (1 August–2 February), and to agistment, grazing on demesne pasture. In 1257, for example, the men of the vill paid 19*s.* for pasturing ahead of the lord's ploughs.[18] There are also numerous examples of illicit pasturing, as in 1407 when seven people presented (accused) by the manor jury included William the shepherd of Eybury, who had brought his flock into the lord's wheat.[19] In 1528 a formal agreement between the steward and 'all tenants and farmers' of the manor stated that in future none would put more than one beast per a. (of holding) into the common fields.[20]

---

9   WAM, 16390.

10   WAM, 16417.

11   WAM, 4870; see Appendix, 77–80.

12   For example: WAM, 16367 (1257), 16400 (1310/11), 1644 (1400–3), 16268 (1442).

13   WAM, 16445 (1403/4), 16334 (1417), 16286 (1520).

14   WAM, 16445, 4870: see 28 above and Appendix, 78, 80; LUCHP, 8, thought that Hyde as acquired by Henry VIII was unwooded but its description was limited to that of the 1520 farm.

15   McMaster, *St Martin*, 254–5, see above, 34.

16   WAM, 16179.

17   WAM, 16288. For Ossul(s)ton common, which seems to have been along Park Lane's roadside verges, see above, 31–2.

18   WAM, 16367; 16444 agistment (1400–3).

19   WAM, 16447 m. 7.

20   WAM, 16449.

The closes that gradually replaced the strips of the open fields still had to be thrown open as lammas lands and it was this loss to permanent inclosures such as Hyde Park that sparked revolts in 1549 and 1592.[21] The issue also remained live outside the park: residents of Kensington were forbidden to common in Westbourne in 1584; in 1599/1600 the manor jury presented a list of 'lamas grownds' that had remained closed; and in 1618 three tenants of lammas lands in Knightsbridge common field were presented, with a steep prospective penalty of 10s. each.[22]

The abbot and subsequently the dean and chapter actually had a park in Knightsbridge, but assuming it stayed in one place it was south of the main road, cannot have been large, and was not a hunting park. The few medieval references always arise from illicit removals, for instance in 1272 when the abbot successfully sued the mayor and sheriff of London for breaking in and removing 80 sheep as a debt settlement, and in 1443 when Richard Huelock (one of the ale-tasters) was presented for breaking into the park 'at Knightsbridge' and taking two oxen.[23] Parks were in all senses defined by their fences. By 1576 the 'common park of Knightsbridge' was 'ruined' and in 1581 a carpenter had sufficiently repaired 'communem parcum vocatum the Sothend of Knightebrige'.[24] In 1585 there was also a new demesne park in Westbourne but by 1592 both were 'decayed' and two different documents register the manor jury's presentment in 1595 that the dean and chapter provided neither a common park (or, in the other document, pound) nor stocks.[25] The later pound was on Knightsbridge Green.[26]

There are no known references to active rabbit warrens but the 1478 demesne description includes Warrenlwey in Knightsbridge and fields in Hyde called Great and Little Conyngger.[27] Two maps produced shortly before the river was widened to create the Long Water and Serpentine show a row of eight ponds along the eastern bank from Bayswater Road down to what would soon become the Serpentine's termination, and it has been assumed that these were medieval fishponds.[28] There are however no references to fish being supplied from here and the river features as a direct abuttal in various medieval land descriptions.[29] Perhaps the ponds were a post-park tidying of the previously marshy area named in 1478 as Long Meadow (Longmedow).[30]

There was demesne land in Southfield: in 1353/4, for example, peas, barley and oats were sown there, the oats in both Upper Shot and Squabbeshot.[31] This demesne was

21   McMaster, *St Martin*, 254–9; the 1592 details are also in Davis, *Knightsbridge*, 15–18.
22   WAM, 16452, 16464–5 (which may also be in Westbourne), 16453 m. 14.
23   WAM, WD f. 93v; Liber Niger f. 4, 16448 m. 1.
24   WAM, 16452 mm. 6, 8.
25   WAM, 16452 m. 11, 16453 mm. 6, 8, 16336.
26   Davis, *Knightsbridge*, 30.
27   WAM, 4870; see Appendix, 78–9, which has minor spelling variations.
28   Henry Wise's 1705 map is reproduced in F. Barker and P. Jackson (eds), *London: 2000 Years of a City and its People* (1974), 163 and LUCHP, 8, 10; for the 1717 map and the assumption, T. Tatton-Brown, 'Kensington and Chelsea in 1717', in F. Barker and P. Jackson (eds), *The History of London in Maps* (1990), 48–9.
29   My thanks to Barbara Harvey for confirming the absence of references. See WAM, 16187, a quitclaim of 1376 for land in Cressewelshot, lying between a ditch (*fossat'*) of the abbot and convent (S) and a ditch called Bayhardeswa[tery]ng (W).
30   Appendix, 78; N. Braybrooke, *London Green* (1959), 82 describes buried stumps from causeways.
31   WAM, 16438: *cultura superior*.

never included in the farm of Hyde and therefore escaped transfer to the Crown, but by 1417 at least 4 a. were farmed, as was 'le quabba' (quagmire) better known as Squabbes, the spring-fed area abutting the main road that also features as demesne meadow and, in 1606, as the source for Robert Fenn's conduit.[32] The process of converting parts of the manor's demesnes and copyhold to freehold had a long history, and in the 16th century the Southfield demesnes (apart from the abbey's park) vanish from the records.

Copyhold, originally the unfree villeins' tenure, stabilised in the later middle ages into land whose title deeds were copies of the transfers recorded in the manor court rolls. The last parts of the Southfield copyhold formed an estate of 44 a. 1 r. regularly described from the 16th century (when closes had replaced most or all of the open field) as 18 a. ½ r. in Southfield, 16 a. 1½ r. in Horseleyes, 3 a. 1½ r. in Squabbes, and 6 a. in Sixacres. These lands were not enfranchised until the mid 19th century, and because of the importance of their eventual buildings are partly considered below.[33] Behind the main road frontage, though, most of the land became part of the Brompton Park Nursery which expanded to cover a considerable cross-border area held through both free- and copyhold ownership and tenancy. The nursery was founded in 1681 by four gardeners including George London and was at its fashionable zenith from 1689 when Henry Wise and London (until his death in 1714) became the partners.[34] It became an essential place to visit and describe, not least because the outing could often be combined with looking at the newly created grounds of nearby Kensington Palace. Queen Anne at her accession in 1702 gave Wise responsibility for all the royal gardens and he was heavily involved in Kensington Gardens' transformation.

After London's death Wise sub-let part of the nursery to two of his gardeners, Joseph Carpenter and William Smith, who carried it forward although it declined in prestige and size thereafter. In 1743 Carpenter surrendered his interest to John Swinhoe who the following year (and described as John Swinhoe of Brompton Park, gentleman) acquired two-thirds of the 44-a. copyhold plus two houses, one of them already his residence.[35] In 1756 Swinhoe surrendered his interest in the nursery to a relative, John Jeffreys, but probably also shrank its lands since when Swinhoe died in 1763 John Jeffreys, nurseryman, was tenant of only 17 of the 30 or so acres.[36] The nursery was finally extinguished after it was acquired for 'South Kensington' in 1852.

32   WAM, 16334; see below, 51.
33   Settlement and Development, 61–3.
34   See *Survey of London*, XXXVIII, 11; Davis, *Knightsbridge*, 132–4; E.J. Willson, *West London Nursery Gardens* (1982), 8–15; LUCKG.
35   WAM, 16459.
36   WAM, 16462; Willson, *West London Nursery Gardens*, 13–14.

Conduits

Water from the many local springs was highly prized.[37] Davis described 'a row of conduits in the fields each side of Rotten Row, whose waters were reached by the one at the end of Parkside, known as St James's, or the Receiving Conduit; and which supplied the royal residences and the Abbey with water'; and it had also included 'a receptacle for its supply to the inhabitants of Knightsbridge'.[38] This is confirmed by two early 18th-century maps, one made to show the abbey's conduit from Hyde Park (1715) and the other the king's conduits into Whitehall and St James (1718).[39] The main heads of both lay close to each other north-east of the Serpentine, with other feeders (and other separate conduits) further east within Hyde Park.

It has been suggested that the abbey's conduit was one of the Benedictine water systems undertaken in the 12th century.[40] If so it is surprising that access for repair was not reserved in the first two surviving demesne farms, for 1358 and 1442, as it was in the third in 1478 (the first known reference) and subsequently in 1487–8 and 1520.[41] The conduit passed to the Crown in 1536 with the rest of Hyde but was specifically returned to the new dean and chapter along with Knightsbridge in 1542, in a grant that also allowed access to the source, 'within our park called Hyde Park viz in a field there anciently called Crosseleyesfeld', presumably a mistake for Cresswell/Carswell.[42] Elizabeth's charter of 1560 is often claimed as a grant but was merely a confirmation.[43] The pipeline was finally severed in 1861 and a wildly inaccurate (but often cited) memorial plaque installed at the site of the conduit house at the north-east corner of the Serpentine in 1870 recorded that 'A supply of water by conduit from this spot was granted to the Abbey of Westminster with the Manor of Hyde by King Edward the Confessor. The Manor was resumed by the Crown in 1536 but the springs as a head and original fountain of water were preserved to the Abbey by the charter of Queen Elizabeth in 1560.'[44]

In 1605 James I granted permission and costs for bringing water 140 paces from a 'mete spring' in Hyde Park to the 'sick, lame and impotent people in our hospital of Knightsbridge ... for the dressing of their meat, and for making condiment potions for their sores'.[45] This is mapped in 1718 as 'Mrs Birkets (sic) Conduit to serve her houses

---

37 For the spring-producing geology see above, 4–5.
38 Davis, *Knightsbridge*, 30–1, 160–1.
39 Both are discussed and the former, WAM, P 11, published in T. Tatton-Brown, 'The Medieval and early Tudor Topography of Westminster', in W. Rodwell and T. Tatton-Brown (eds), *Westminster I: The Art, Architecture and Archaeology of the Royal Abbey*, BAA Conference Trans. XXXIX Pt I (2015), 13. See also below, n. 46. I am very grateful to the author for sharing both maps with me ahead of the publication.
40 T. Tatton-Brown, 'Water Supply', The Westminster Abbey Chorister 55 (Winter 2012/3), 39–43; but, after discussion, in 'The Med. and early Tudor Topog. of Westminster', 12, he avoids making a direct early link to this part of the system.
41 WAM, 16265, 16268, 4870; Reg. Bk I ff. 20, 33, Reg. Bk II ff. 154v–155.
42 WAM, LXXXIII, *L&P Henry VIII*, vol. XVII, no. 714, 392–6, Knightsbridge at 392, conduit at 396 where Crosseleyesfeld is given as Crosse Leysefelde.
43 *Cal. Pat. Eliz.* 1558–60, 402.
44 The texts of this and a second plaque (stolen in 2012) are transcribed in Tatton-Brown, 'Water Supply', 39.
45 BL, Add. MSS 5775, quoted in Davis, *Knightsbridge*, 52–4.

at Knightsbridge'.[46] Robert Fenn received permission to build a conduit and pipes at Squabbes in 1606, with a description providing running English translations of the key words: 'vaults and cesterns of brick' and 'channeles and troughes of brick and lead' for drawing together the water running, lying and being in the close.[47] Two more conduits were just outside the area but relevant to it. The pipe built in 1439 to bring water to London from a group of springs in Ox Lese in Paddington was not allowed to cross Hyde but ran under the eventual north-eastern corner of Hyde Park, a discrepancy that provoked some of the earliest speculation about the relationship of the manor and park.[48] The marble conduit on the Kensington side of the border mentioned in some of the Coppin/Finch documents had been constructed to take water to Henry VIII's children's nursery in Chelsea.[49]

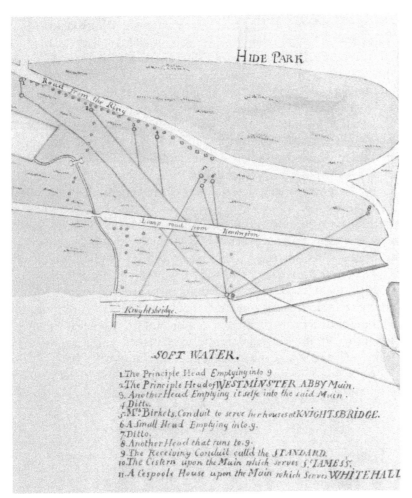

Map 7 *The Hyde Park section of 'A Survey of the Conduits etc. to Whitehall, St. James's etc 1718'.*

46   See Map 7; the BL has two copies of this survey: Maps K. Top. 21. 1.3 and Maps Crace Port 12.34. The Birkheads held the hospital site, the later Parkside: see below, 69, and *Survey of London*, XLV, 37–42.

47   WAM, 16453 m. 11.

48   Davis, 'Conduit System', 53–8; London CC (G.L. Gomme), *Tyburn Gallows* (1909).

49   Faulkner, *Kensington*, 406.

Settlement and Development

Three masterful *Survey of London* volumes cover Knightsbridge's development, but almost entirely from the 17th century onwards and without using manorial records.[50] This section therefore concentrates on the earlier picture, some later manorial evidence and the influence of the park.

Early Development

Knightsbridge excluding Westbourne had only one hamlet, which began at the bridge and continued west along the main road, and since the road and bridge were its *raison d'être*, it always had a commercial focus. The earliest deeds, undated but 13th century, feature a smithy and at least two other buildings in a row on the north side of the road immediately west of the bridge. Firstly Henry, son of Gilbert of the Bridge (*ponte*) of Knightsbridge, granted Geoffrey Smith (*faber*) a plot of land on which Geoffrey's smithy stood.[51] Then in the next generation Geoffrey's son John granted Martin Smith a messuage lying between one that Henry of the Bridge was letting to the abbey's Lady Chapel (west), the small watercourse running under the bridge of Knightsbridge (east), and the road (south).[52] Henry later changed the lease to a grant in which the messuage was described as lying between those of Martin Smith and William le Blaur.[53] The first two documents give the plot sizes, and although these were small they were presumably behind the roadside verges, the manorial waste from which small plots were later granted.

The abbey at this period was voraciously acquisitive and in 1283x1307 William Smith transferred a house and, separately, a plot between his tenement and that of Juliana in the Lane, three of whose houses were also later transferred.[54] In 1311 William granted his messuage and half its garden near the stream to his son Michael, but the Knightsbridge *serviens'* account for 1310/11 includes 3s. 8d. from farming three houses formerly William's.[55] The accounts give indications of commercial life. By 1328/9 the smith's house was farmed for 2s. and the smithy for a substantial 6s. but the following year no tenant could be found for the smithy.[56] In the 1330s the smithy was tenanted, still at 6s., but the house had vanished from the list of farms, and in 1339/40 eight shops make their first appearance.[57] The number of shops fluctuated thereafter but settled at five in the 1350s.[58] By 1353/4 Laurence Smith was paying 8s. for a house and smithy 'standing in the middle

---

50 *Survey of London*, XXXVIII, XLI, XLV; *VCH Middx*, XIII ignores Knightsbridge in its section on settlement.
51 WAM, 16195, WD ff. 564v–565: *placea, fabrica*.
52 WAM, 16249: *parvum ductum*.
53 WAM, 16196 and WD f. 565.
54 WAM, 16261, 16246, 16400; Harvey, *WA Estates*.
55 WAM, 16230, 16400.
56 WAM, 16417–8.
57 WAM, 16419–16422; there is a gap between 16421 (1336–7) and 16422 (1339–40).
58 WAM, 16423–16443.

of the road' and 13s. 4d. for what was presumably a separate smithy.[59] The account run ends in 1358 and smithies and shops are largely absent from later, more spasmodic records, although in 1375 Thomas Smyth was granted two 'shoppes in la Newrente' for life.[60] There are other glimpses of growth: a 1474 lease included a messuage on the Green and a newly-built house (*tenementum*) abutting south on the road.[61] And, east of the bridge, the lazarhouse grant of 1466 shows the first known exploitation of the roadside waste.[62]

The number of 14th-century shops is interesting but even allowing for fragmentary records these are slim pickings, particularly compared to urbanised central Westminster.[63] Davis mentions a Thursday cattle market held on Knightsbridge Green until the start of the 19th century and an annual fair on 31 July but apparently without knowing any detail.[64] Given London's 14th-century edicts on butchery it would be reasonable to expect activities similar to those on the Great North Road at Chipping Barnet, but at Knightsbridge no butchers appear in court rolls for leaving entrails inappropriately and there are no obvious traces of an early cattle market or fair.[65] Barnet's Middle Row was a standard early development from market stalls, Knightsbridge's 'a medley of very inferior houses' not built until the 1720s.[66]

Inns

Knightsbridge later became famous or infamous for its inns but in the court rolls that survive between 1358 and 1443 the ale-tasters regularly presented only one to three illicit brewers and a couple of regraters (resale at undue profit), the same names constantly recurring; none was from Westbourne but these are minuscule numbers.[67] By 1511–29 and the next surviving rolls things were clearly changing: the regraters had vanished but the number and variety of brewers and bakers was starting to grow.[68] In 1519, for example, all three bakers were allegedly 'forinsec' (outsiders) and selling at short weight, and all six brewers (*pandaxatores*) were also allegedly forinsec and included one from St Martin-in-the-Fields, two from Kensington and one from Brentford. Again many of the same names recur for years, among them two alewives, Christiana Norrys, a widow sometimes categorised as forinsec, and Agnes Mewtes who with her husband held a substantial estate in Southfield.[69] On occasion the ale-taster was also among the malefactors.

By 1511 a distinction was being made between two types of brewer, *pandoxatores* and *tiplatores*, with the latter fined smaller amounts. In 1522 John Rolbysley paid an entry

59   WAM, 16438: *in media strata*.
60   WAM, 16446.
61   WAM, 16179.
62   WAM, 16335; see above and below, 31, 68.
63   Cf Rosser, *Medieval W* and G. Rosser, 'London and Westminster: the Suburb in the Urban Economy in the Later Middle Ages', in J.A.F. Thomson (ed.), *Towns and Townspeople in the Fifteenth Century* (1989), 45–61.
64   Davis, *Knightsbridge*, 145–6.
65   Ibid., 32–3 (1361); Chancellor, *Knightsbridge*, 7 (1371, 1379/80); P. Taylor, *Barnet and Hadley Past* (2002), 19–28.
66   Davis, *Knightsbridge*, 144; *Survey of London*, XLV, 88.
67   WAM, 16446–8.
68   WAM, 16449 covers various years between 1511–29.
69   On the estate see below, 61.

fine as custodian of the *tiplacio et hospicio* at the sign of the Rose. He was presumably the John Rollesley presented with three other *tiplatores* in 1518 but is not on any of the other surviving lists, which perhaps suggests that presentments could be for actual contraventions rather than simply a covert tax. The Rose reappears in 1576 when Thomas Haselwood was given permission to erect a piece of wood called 'a poste' in the king's highway and affix 'the signe of the rose' to it.[70] Both these previously undiscovered references are unique and Davis thought that the Rose, later the Rose & Crown, which stood on the south side of the road near the Green, was (by 1859) some 300 years old, the oldest house in Knightsbridge and formerly its largest inn; a date of 1679 was discovered when it was pulled down in the 1870s, but this clearly came from a rebuilding.[71]

It is impossible to establish the inns' chronology, although the numbers presumably grew as long-distance travel increased. Among the inns demolished in the 1840s for Albert Gate were the Queen's Head, where brickwork dated 1576 was found, and the White Hart within the site of the former hospital.[72] The White Hart that features in the Coppin/Finch deeds between 1619 and 1662 was at the manor and parish's western end, close to Kensington village, and by 1662 had acquired a row of newly-built neighbours.[73] Davis provides the usual 18th-century tales of highwaymen in collusion with innkeepers, and as well as the main road other helpful post-medieval elements were Knightsbridge chapel's brisk trade in clandestine marriages (see below) and the park's proximity.[74]

Hyde Park's Influence

Ever since its creation Hyde Park has been a major factor. Its formation in the 1530s probably involved demolishing roadside houses and certainly destroyed the manor house at Hyde and any other buildings along the vanished lanes of what had until then been the hamlet's northern hinterland. All future development on the north was restricted to at most a narrow strip and this must permanently have affected the hamlet's focus, pushing it towards the southern side of the road and therefore eventually encouraging its cross-border spread. There have also been other significant, sometimes conflicting, commercial and residential impacts. After Charles I, *c.*1630, opened part of the park to society's upper echelons it developed into a major area of elite entertainment, with some knock-on benefits.[75] Pepys in 1665 'did … away out of the park to Knightsbridge and there ate and drank in the coach and so home'.[76] In 1669 he arrived before the park was open, 'so went to Knightsbridge and there ate and drank at the World's End', an inn later called the Fulham Bridge on the Brompton Road and from the 1770s at the Sloane Street junction.[77] Broadening the area's attractions, Spring Garden(s) opened *c.*1670, a house with a pleasure garden that lasted in various guises down to the early 19th century; Harvey Nichols occupies part of the site.[78]

70   WAM, 16452 m. 6.
71   Davis, *Knightsbridge*, 103–4; *Survey of London*, XLV, 78–9.
72   Davis, *Knightsbridge*, 163; *Survey of London*, XLV, 37, 47.
73   See above, 43; TNA, C 54/4097/33.
74   Davis, *Knightsbridge*, 28–9; *Survey of London*, XLV, 3.
75   Merritt, *W (2)*, 212–8; LUCHP, 9–11.
76   Davis, *Knightsbridge*, 150.
77   Ibid., 150–1; *Survey of London*, XXXVII, 3, 33–5.
78   *Survey of London*, XLV, 30–2; Davis, *Knightsbridge*, 149–53, 155–8, conflates it with the World's End.

Figure 13 *Until the 19th century Hyde Park's only entry was at Hyde Park Corner but Decimus Burton's grand Screen was not opened until 1829.*

The park was also used for military purposes and in logical extension stables built south-west of Hyde Park Corner *c.*1760 were foot barracks from *c.*1789 to the 1840s.[79] Knightsbridge cavalry barracks were built on the roadside strip at the hamlet's western edge in 1792, rebuilt in 1878 and again in 1967, this time with a tower that spoils the views across Hyde Park; relocation and demolition were under discussion in 2015.[80] Soldiers from both establishments were customers for all local amusements.[81] Cavalrymen and riders in Hyde Park help explain both the area for exercising and showing horses attached to the World's End by the 1770s and the location of Tattersalls, the great horse auctioneers, which opened near Hyde Park Corner in 1766 and moved to premises below Knightsbridge Green in 1864, remaining until the outbreak of the Second World War.[82]

79   *Survey of London*, XLV, 23–4.
80   Ibid., XLV, 64–76; *Archit. Jnl*: http://www.architectsjournal.co.uk/news/daily-news/listing-refused-minister-ignores-he-on-spences-hyde-park-barracks/8689810.article (accessed 14 Oct. 2015).
81   Davis, *Knightsbridge*, 41–7; *Survey of London*, XLV, 23–4.
82   *Survey of London*, XLI, 5, 34–5; XLV, 89–91.

Settlement from *c.*1600

Poor Residents

Providing services to the wealthy is seldom a path to riches and until well into the 19th century most Knightsbridge residents were poor. Tracing the detail through the early modern period is, however, unusually difficult. In 1616 and 1618 the manor jury reported that cottagers were illicitly taking lodgers ('Anglice, inmates'), a sure sign, but the further statement that the constable or headboroughs would permanently forfeit their roles if they 'shall have notice of an Inmate and not acqueynt the churchwardens and collectors of the parishe, To thende that [they] may take Suertyes' perfectly captures the general transfer of powers from manors to parishes.[83] Ensuring that all residents were under mutual surety had been the essence of the view of frankpledge, part of the main and by 1511 usually sole (albeit busy) annual court.[84] But by 1597/8 although the courts were still significant no court with view had been held for three years.[85]

Parish records usually compensate for the manors' decline but Knightsbridge had only a chapel with no civil powers and (needles and haystacks apart) it is far from certain that the records of St Margaret's and St Martin's flag their Knightsbridge entries reliably, or fully distinguish between the ordinary inhabitants and those in the hospital (technically in St Martin's) who were drawn from a wider area.[86] Poor relief was certainly distributed beyond the hospital during visits from the mother parishes in the late 16th and 17th centuries.[87] During the Interregnum Knightsbridge's inhabitants petitioned for chapel repair money, claiming that most of the 68 or so local families were 'very poore laboringe people' and 'Those who formerly were good Benefactors are many dead and the rest have left us'.[88]

Wealthy Residents

Who these good benefactors were, where they resided, and whether overt Royalists had left are all interesting questions. Outsiders were active from at least the 13th century in the local land market, but apart from the owners of the Hyde house it is seldom clear if they chose to live locally, or if so exactly where. The market burgeoned generally in the 16th century, when Hyde Park coincidentally reduced the available land and perhaps stimulated interest in the adjacent area. Three estates particularly affected later development. Sir George Coppin's land immediately west of Hyde Park is one, its subsequent royal purchase preventing standard development. The others were those of Sir William Blake and Sir Robert Fenn(e), both of them cross-border and both therefore divided between *Survey of London* volumes.

83   WAM, 16453 mm. 13–14.
84   WAM, 16449.
85   WAM, 40627.
86   Cf J.V. Kitto, *St Martin-in-the-Fields. The Accounts of the Churchwardens 1525–1603* (1901) and see below, Knightsbridge Leper Hospital and Chapel, 67–73.
87   Davis, *Knightsbridge*, 50 (St Margaret's, 1595, 1597); Merritt, *W (1)*, 210 (St Martin's, late 1610s and early 1620s).
88   *Survey of London*, XLV, 41.

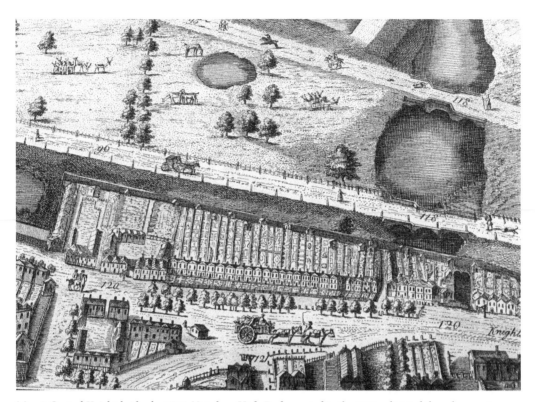

Map 8 *Central Knightsbridge by 1766. Note how Hyde Park, created in the 1530s, dictated the subsequent settlement shape.*

Blake and Moreau Estates

Knightsbridge from the hamlet west to Ennismore Gardens

Sir William Blake, citizen and vintner, bought and moved into Hale House in Brompton in 1606 and most of his subsequently acquired estate was in Kensington.[89] Nevertheless the inquisition post mortem in 1630 reported 100 a. of meadow and pasture 'in St Margaret Westminster, Chelsea, Knightsbridge and Kensington' plus, in Knightsbridge, the Rose, a messuage and 120 a. occupied by one Tannett, and a messuage and 10 a. occupied by Easton and Farmer.[90] If the figures are accurate he must have held virtually the whole area between Knightsbridge Green and today's Ennismore Gardens. Since his Knightsbridge lands were all freehold Blake only features in the extant court rolls in 1638, when he was in default of suit and owed 20-years' back rent of 1*d.* per annum (both freehold obligations).[91] He had acquired the Rose, various closes, gardens and acres in the common field from Robert Pepper for £480 in 1611 and a milk house at the southern end of the Rose's yard plus part of Pepper's orchard for £35 in 1613.[92]

89   Cf *Survey of London*, XXXVIII, XLI, XLV.
90   Additions to the illustrated Faulkner, BL, L.R. 271 c.3, between pp. 440–1.
91   WAM, 16453 m. 16.
92   Additions to the illustrated Faulkner, BL, L.R. 271 c.3, between pp. 440–1.

Figure 14 *The Paxton's Head. An inn has flourished on this site since at least 1632.*

Blake's estate was gradually dismembered and in 1705 Philip Moreau (1656–1733) bought one of the Knightsbridge houses and moved in; lying immediately south-west of the Green, it later became Grosvenor House and was demolished c.1864 for Tattersalls.[93] Moreau added more of Blake's Knightsbridge land in 1718.[94] He first appears in the court rolls in 1724, as a juror by virtue of his sole copyhold, the Red Lion on the main road at Knightsbridge Green.[95] By 1632 called the King's Arms, then the Golden Lion, this became the Sun in 1748x1757, the Granby Head in 1765x1789, and is currently the Paxton's Head.[96] Beneath the re-namings and rebuildings (the current version is c.1900), this is the sole survivor of Knightsbridge's earlier inns; whether the messuage built on Knightsbridge Green by 1474 was its precursor is unclear.[97] Moreau also bought most of Knightsbridge Green and soon built the first part of Middle Row, the initial stage in the Green's development.[98] His estate was dispersed after 1759 but fully covering the Green took more than a century longer.[99]

Development west along the main road began with a string of grand houses set in generous grounds.[100] Running westward, these were Powis House (c.1689–1811), Kent House (1793–1870), Stratheden House (1772–c.1900) and Rutland House (1753–1836),

---

93 *Survey of London*, XLV, 77–8, 88–9.
94 Ibid., XLV, 77, citing XXXXVIII and XLI, says he acquired all Blake's Knightsbridge land, but limits Blake's estate to the cross-border 100 a.
95 It was surrendered by George and Maria Pomfret to Henry Hawkes as mortgage surety in 1689 and passed to Hawkes' co-heirs in 1704: WAM, 16455.
96 WAM, 16454 (1667, 1679), 16456 (1724), 16438 (1736), 16459 (1748), 16460 (1757), 16462 (1763, 1765), 16463 (1789); *Survey of London*, XLV, 77, 79–81.
97 WAM, 16179.
98 *Survey of London*, XLV, 77 and passim.
99 Ibid., XLV, 88.
100 The following detail is from ibid.; for additional social detail see Davis, *Knightsbridge*.

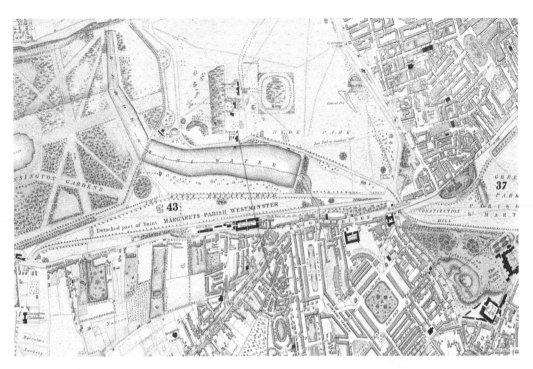

Map 9 *Extract from Greenwood's Map of London, 1854, showing the development along the southern side of Knightsbridge between Brompton Road and Gore.*

whose owners and occupiers included royal and ducal mistresses, other aristocrats, politicians and people connected with the theatre. It was they who gave Knightsbridge a new tone and cachet but even so they never had things entirely their own way. By the late 18th century there was a floorcloth manufactory immediately west of Powis House, whose charms were also lessened when the barracks were built opposite in the 1790s, blocking the view to the park. The house and its grounds were replaced by the streets of the Trevor estate, aimed at the moderately prosperous middle class but in fact a lodging house district until the early 20th century. The factory closed *c.*1888 but the building had a range of other uses, skating club, exhibition centre, car hire depot, until demolition in the 1970s. Safely more distant from the hamlet and its influences, Rutland House was replaced by upmarket Rutland Gate which continued attracting high-class occupants, as did the later replacements of Kent and Stratheden Houses, which also included flats.

Behind the main road, the Montpelier Square area was developed from the 1820s; its centre immediately (and enduringly) appealed to politicians and the literati, and its working class cottage fringes moved rapidly upmarket in the 1920s. Raphael Street was built from the 1840s for respectable working class occupiers, but they disliked the noise from places of entertainment and the street deteriorated into low-end lodging houses; there were frequent prosecutions for brothel-keeping, an activity blamed on the barracks. The houses were pulled down in 1956–7 for the office development that destroyed much of the Knightsbridge Green area.

Figure 15 (above) *Nos 10–22 Rutland Gate, built on part of the Rutland House site in 1838.*

Figure 16 (below) *Rutland Court, flats built in 1901–3 on the site of Stratheden House.*

Sir Robert Fenn's Estate

Knightsbridge from Ennismore Gardens west to Gore and 'South Kensington'

West of the Blake and Moreau accumulations was the other major 16th/17th-century estate, that of Sir Robert Fenn, covering in modern terms the area from Ennismore Gardens to the Royal Albert Hall and split between the *Survey of London* volumes for Knightsbridge and the Museums Area of South Kensington. Fenn himself only appears in the latter, with the statement that in the mid 17th century Sir Robert, Charles I's Clerk of the Green Cloth, held what became the 1851 Commissioners' Gore House estate within his larger free- and copyhold estate.[101] The Knightsbridge copyhold (partly discussed under Agriculture) covered 44 a. 1 r., most of it unenfranchised until the mid 19th century, and the transfers were entered in the manor court rolls down to the final roll in 1797. (Soon after the Restoration, in 1660, recording the copyhold transfers became the courts' sole activity.) The rolls were not explored for the *Survey* volumes and they supply useful additional detail both before and after the Fenns.

The 44 a. 1 r. constituted a unit well before it came to Sir Robert. In 1524 John Mewtes, who had held the lands jointly with his first wife, Agnes, transferred them to himself and his second wife, Leticia, and their joint heirs or in default to hers.[102] They passed from Leticia Greenfield at her death in 1572 to her son Gentilis, at whose death in 1592 Alice Fenn, wife of Robert, was admitted as Gentilis's heir, and inheritance was immediately transferred from her heirs to Robert's.[103] In 1606 Robert was given permission to make a conduit at Squabbes and also to demise (let) Squabbes and a close called Middle Gore for 99 years.[104] He died in 1618 and the land descended to his son, also Robert.[105]

In 1620 this Robert, who is the one cited by the *Survey of London*, headed the list of Kensington residents warned to attend the Knightsbridge court.[106] He in turn died in 1660, leaving the land in trust for his daughter Rebecca Walthew, after whose death, and a complicated recovery against the trustees, her son Edmund Walthew was admitted in November 1674.[107] On 8 December Edmund split the estate, transferring to its tenant, Humphrey Tomlinson, a third or 14 a. 2 r. 25 p., namely Squabbes (3 a. 2 r. 36 p.), Middle Gore (8 a. 1 r. 4 p.) and land extracted from 'Anglice the West part of the South Field' (2a. 2r. 25 p.), with Squabbes abutting north on the main road and the other abuttals Edmund's lands and Tomlinson's freeholds.[108]

The court rolls add little for the descent of this third, described from other sources in the *Survey of London*: it passed through Tomlinson's daughter Anne Busby to his grandson Tomlinson Busby, remaining with the Busbys until 1820 when it passed to the

101 *Survey of London*, XXXVIII, 11. Knighted in 1641, he was Clerk Comptroller from 1638–43 and reinstated in 1660: J.C. Sainty, 'Officers of the Green Cloth: Clerks and Clerk Comptrollers', 1999, http://www.history.ac.uk/publications/office/greencloth.html (accessed 6 Jan. 2016).

102 WAM, 16449.

103 WAM, 16452 m. 3, 16453 mm. 6–7; Alice had previously been married to Thomas Holmes: for other Holmes and Greenfield involvement see WAM, 16452 m. 6 (1576), 16467 m. 3 (1596).

104 WAM, 16453 m. 11; for the conduit see also above, 51.

105 WAM, 16453 m. 14.

106 WAM, 16466.

107 WAM, 16454 mm. 1–2, 4.

108 WAM, 16454 m. 4; *Survey of London*, XXXVIII, 11–12.

Aldridges.[109] The rolls do however say that in 1685 Anne's copyhold inheritance included a house occupied by John Bond, and that by 1744 the estate included several houses lately erected at Gore.[110] Which exactly these were is unclear. The two major houses in the area were ultimately Grove House, which replaced an earlier dwelling shortly before 1750, and Gore House but to either side of these were some lesser houses.[111] Immediately east of the boundary stood Hyde Park Terrace, which was rebuilt c.1829 (and destroyed c.1960 for the Royal College of Art). Just east of Gore House, within the Greenwood map's Upper Kensington Gore, Davis described some of the mid 19th-century occupants of Mercer House and a 'row of five houses called emphatically Kensington Gore', but neither he nor the *Survey of London* gives any building detail.[112] Gore House's tenants included William Wilberforce and Lady Blessington, whose very different salons attracted widespread fame.[113] All these houses were purchased by the 1851 Commissioners as part of the (newly-named) Gore House estate and demolished for 'South Kensington'.

The court rolls offer rather more new detail for the two-thirds of the estate briefly retained by Walthew.[114] In 1682 he transferred it to Henry Hassard of Kensington, whose grandson, also Henry Hassard, transferred it in 1744 to John Swinhoe of Brompton Park together with two houses, one newly built and already occupied by John and the other occupied by William Lowther (not to be confused with a later namesake).[115] In February 1757 Swinhoe transferred 3 a. 'whereon a certain messuage ... is very lately erected' to Elizabeth Chudleigh, mistress and from 1769 illegitimately wife of Evelyn Pierrepont, 2nd duke of Kingston.[116] This became Kingston House, whose estate was enlarged in 1759 by Elizabeth's purchase of two freehold fields to the east, hitherto the westernmost part of the Moreau estate, and by the duke's purchase from Swinhoe of a further 4 a. 1 r. 5 p. of the copyhold lying between Chudleigh's brick wall (east) and the garden pales of Elizabeth Harrison (west).[117]

At Swinhoe's death in 1763 his widow, Arabella, claimed the Swinhoe residence for life with joint descent to the children of their daughter, Hortensia Searle, plus 17 a. of copyhold in the tenure of John Jeffreys nurseryman to the uses of Swinhoe's will; the other daughter, Lucy Swinhoe, claimed the house occupied by Elizabeth Harrison.[118] John and Arabella's residence, adjacent to Busby's grounds, was sold in the 1840s to George Eden, earl of Auckland, and became known as Eden Lodge. It eluded the 1851 Commissioners, whose rectangle between the main road, Exhibition Road, Cromwell Road and Queen's Gate it would have completed, and was instead sold after the death of Emily Eden in 1869 to William Lowther; he sold the southern part of the grounds for Lowther Gardens and replaced the house with Lowther Lodge, since 1912 the home

109 *Survey of London*, XXXVIII, 11.
110 WAM, 16454 mm. 7v–9, 16459.
111 *Survey of London*, XXXVIII, 11–15.
112 Davis, *Knightsbridge*, 131–2; see also above, 21–2 and Map 9, 59.
113 Ibid., XXXVIII, 12; Davis, *Knightsbridge*, 136–42.
114 *Survey of London*, XXXVIII, 13–15 and XLV, chs 9–10.
115 WAM, 16454 m. 4v, 16459.
116 WAM, 16460.
117 WAM, 16461; *Survey of London*, XLV, 157.
118 WAM, 16462.

Figure 17 *Lowther Lodge, built in 1873–5 and since 1912 the home of the Royal Geographical Society.*

of the Royal Geographical Society.[119] Lucy Swinhoe's inheritance was Park House, built by her father in 1753 and demolished in the 1850s by C.J. Freake, who also bought the 11½ -a. rump of the Brompton Park estate and set about developing Prince's Gate and Prince's Gardens.[120] Kingston House, demolished in the 1930s, was the last survivor but its grounds gave way to Prince's Gate in 1851–5 and Ennismore Gardens from the 1860s; when these houses too became over-large they were partly replaced by flats and, later, townhouses.[121] Once the crowd-pulling Great Exhibition of 1851 was over, all these developments profited from their proximity to the park.

Despite the elite houses, in 1848 most of the hamlet's *c*.5,000 inhabitants were still working class and living in crowded conditions near the barracks.[122] The mid-century developments ratcheted up the tension between suburban newcomers and the area's flourishing commercial outlets, whose success was routinely blamed on the barracks even though Knightsbridge had always been a way-station. The loss of coach travellers of all classes had also been partly offset by wider access to the park, both social and, with the opening of Albert Gate in 1845, physical.[123] As late as the 1860s the High Road presented 'a succession of music-halls, taverns, beer stores, oyster saloons and cheap tobacconists'.[124] Suburban values triumphed and this stretch was swept away in the 1870s, when the barracks were also rebuilt and the road widened.

119 *Survey of London*, XXXVIII, 13–14, 57, 327–31.
120 Ibid., XLV, ch. 10; on Freake also *Survey of London*, XXXVIII, passim.
121 Ibid., XLV, 5, ch. 9.
122 Ibid., XLV, 9–10, 16.
123 On the gates, ibid., XLV, 6–9, 47–9; Pevsner, *Westminster*, 662–3.
124 *Survey of London*, XLV, 5, 79–80.

Development East of the Hamlet

East of the hamlet, Lowndes Terrace was built in the 1820s between William Street and Sloane Street and was on the manor's narrow roadside strip even though the rest of the Lowndes development was in Chelsea.[125] Belgravia is often taken to cover the whole area between Hyde Park Corner and Sloane Street, but it was actually developed by the Grosvenor estate within Eye and therefore stops at the now-hidden Westbourne, just east of William Street and Lowndes Square. In developmental terms this made very little difference since the Lowndes development occurred at the same time and co-operatively, but extending 'Belgravia' to include Knightsbridge deepens confusion.[126]

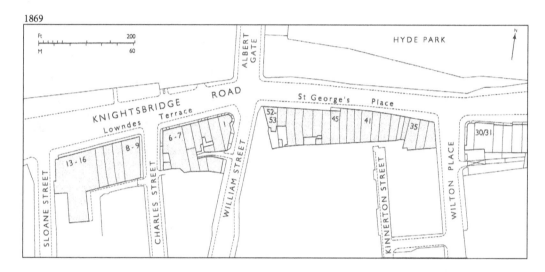

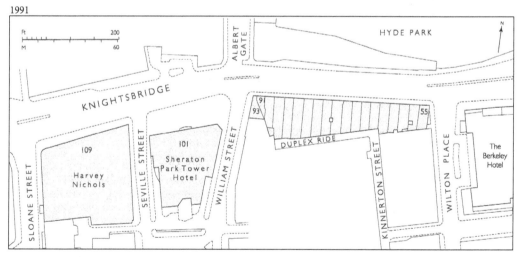

Map 10 *Knightsbridge, south side between Wilton Place and Sloane Street in 1869 and 1991.*

125 Ibid., XLV, 19, 31–3.
126 Pevsner, *Westminster*, 727–55.

Figure 18 *Harvey Nichols department store.*

The Lowndes development replaced Spring Gardens (which had usually been referred to as Knightsbridge) and Lowndes Terrace at one stage housed two of the three great department stores that became key to Knightsbridge's modern self-definition.[127] Benjamin Harvey opened his shop at the Sloane Street corner in 1831 and by 1878 what was now Harvey Nichols occupying the whole terrace up to Seville Street. Sloane Street properties were added in the 1880s, the whole site was rebuilt in 1889–94 and there have been successive modifications both before and since its acquisition by Debenhams in 1920. Woollands' initial trajectory was similar, starting in one shop in 1869, occupying the whole eastern part of the terrace by 1892, completely rebuilt in 1896–1901 and acquired by Debenhams in 1949; but it was demolished for the Sheraton Park Tower Hotel in 1967. 'Harrods of Knightsbridge', on the south side of Brompton Road, has always been in Kensington. Charles Harrod began expanding his father's grocery here *c.*1860 and a fire in 1883 encouraged the rebuild.[128] Harrod's start coincided with the upgrading of Brompton Road and both were factors in Knightsbridge's shift of focus.

127 For this and the following paragraph, *Survey of London*, XLV, 31–6.
128 Ibid., XLI, 17–23.

Figure 19 *No. 1 Hyde Park, taken from South Carriage Drive and looking east. Edinburgh Gate and Epstein's site-specific sculpture have been relocated to the development's western end.*

Re-development in the 20th and 21st Centuries

There was a lot of 20th-century rebuilding, with the 1950s contributions, the office blocks around Knightsbridge Green, Bowater House with Edinburgh Gate, and the demolition of Parkside for road widening, particularly destructive of earlier (or indeed any) character.[129] Nevertheless after the Second World War Knightsbridge became an increasingly desirable address, and as air travel grew the easy access to Heathrow airport accentuated its appeal. Since the most recent local *Survey of London* (2000) it has become even more an enclave of the international super-rich, attracted, perhaps, by shops rather than parks or museums. Buildings are being replaced accordingly and one of the most recent, entirely symptomatic additions is the Candy Brothers' No 1 Hyde Park (2011), which has replaced the Bowater House/Edinburgh Gate block and is therefore, as it happens, within Knightsbridge proper.

129 *Survey of London*, XLV, 92–4, 59, 40.

The Knightsbridge Leper Hospital and Chapel

KNIGHTSBRIDGE CHAPEL WAS ORIGINALLY part of the leper hospital which lay immediately east of the bridge.[1] Both have been covered in other publications, so within a brief outline this account concentrates on points that are either newly found or particularly relevant in terms of Knightsbridge's identity.

The Hospital

Marjorie Honeybourne, the first historian to examine the leper hospitals on main roads on the outskirts of London, thought that Knightsbridge had probably been set up or taken over by the City in the 13th or 14th century.[2] More recently Patricia Croot discovered a chancery case of c.1485 that appeared to show it had been founded by two lepers, William Thomson and his wife Agnes, 'shortly before 1474'.[3] The case stated that Agnes had held a leasehold plot acquired by her previous husband, John Simonds, from the abbey and that because she and Thomson wished to build a small chapel they had asked Henry Clowe (spellings vary) to negotiate a longer term. The successful result was the abbot's 80-year lease of land at Knightsbridge called Lazarcotes made on 23 March 1473 to Henry and Thomas Clowgh and Richard Thomson, by which William, Agnes and their son Richard had the use for life with remainder to Henry to use the property to house the sick.[4] Thomson's will, made in 1474, takes the same line and by 1485, with all three Thomsons dead, Henry was in charge of the hospital and chapel.[5] He bequeathed it to his sons-in-law Robert Elyngton and William Campion in May 1512, and in June Robert acquired a new lease.[6] This pattern of control, with its inherent risk that family or financial interest could outweigh medical expertise, was therefore established from the start.

The start, though, was not exactly as the c.1485 account portrayed it. The rental of Knightsbridge rents payable to the warden of the new work was updated in April 1474

---

1   Pevsner, *Westminster*, 755, mistakenly places it west of the bridge.
2   Honeybourne, 'Leper Hospitals', 38; *Religious Houses*, 322–3, provides an updated summary.
3   *Religious Houses*, 322, citing TNA, C 1/52/274–7.
4   WAM, 16298. It is cited in *Survey of London*, XLV, 40 but omitting Henry, and thence in *Religious Houses*, 322.
5   *Religious Houses*, 322.
6   TNA, PROB 11/17/215, cited in *Religious Houses*, 322. The lease is WAM, 16284, also in Reg. Bk II f. 39, but Elyngton is not in *Religious Houses*' list of governors, 323.

but, very luckily, instead of following the 1473 lease it describes the previous situation.[7] John Symonds was holding by copy of a (now-vanished) 1466 court roll a parcel of wasteland in Knightsbridge on which he had built a leper house; the parcel measured (in perches) 10 in length from the leper house ditch on the east to the bridge called Knightsbridge on the west, 4 in width up to the king's highway on the west and 3¾ on the east. The term was 51 years and the rent 2s. Credit for founding the leper house therefore belongs to Symonds, not Thomson. For reasons discussed above the waste was granted via Knightsbridge manor and the land, hospital and chapel were always referred to simply as Knightsbridge even though they were east of the bridge.

The 1473 lease, while somehow failing to mention the Thomsons' life interest, shows some significant changes.[8] The plot size was greatly enlarged to (again in perches) 24 in length on the south, 17¼ in width on the west, 1½ in width on the north from the edge of the garden, 40 in length on the west and north and 1 in width on the east. This plot presumably went beyond the manorial waste and the lease apparently removed Lazarcotes from the copyhold category: subsequent transfers are traced through leases and the Register Books not through court rolls.[9] The rent was also doubled (and stayed at 4s. at least until 1641) and the term lengthened. The site still abutted the highway on the south and certainly until the 1512 renewal and presumably until the park's creation was surrounded by abbey lands on the other three sides.[10]

The hospital's guider complained in 1595 that 'There was a certen pece of grounde belonginge there unto, which was taken awaye and inclosed into Hide Parke'.[11] The hospital's site may perhaps have been trimmed (none of the post-park leases gives dimensions) or perhaps the loss was the three-foot wide 'bank or parcel of land' reserved from some of the Hyde leases for carrying timber 'for repair of les lazarcotes'.[12] But there is no other sign of any separate pre-park endowment. Great and Little Spittle Meadow, which lay on both banks of the river in Eye and Chelsea and eventually formed part of the Lowndes estate, have been suggested but had actually belonged to St James's Hospital.[13] The St James's estate removed from Eton College in 1531 included an outlying 18 a. 'at a bridge called Knightsbridge' and in early 16th-century Knightsbridge court rolls the Master of St James' featured for failing to scour ditches southward from the bridge.[14] Seven of the acres went into the park but the Spittle Meadows were too far south.

Knightsbridge hospital did in 1606 receive a piece of ground 'on the south side of the high waye right against the hospitall' measuring 193 ft on the north, 184 ft on the south, 63 ft on the east and 77 ft on the west, which according to evidence provided in 1576

7   WAM, 16355.
8   WAM, 16298.
9   Leases from 1512–1654 are within WAM, 16284–16307 and other 16th- and 17th-century material relating to the lazarhouse within WAM, 16311–16320. For renewals via the Register Book entries see C.S. Knighton, *Acts of the Dean and Chapter of Westminster Parts 1–2 1543–1509, Part 3 1609–42* (WA Records Ser. 1997, 1999, 2006).
10   1512: WAM, 16284 and Reg. Bk II f. 39; same measurements in 1533: WAM, Reg. Bk II f. 294.
11   WAM, 16311, cited by Lysons and thence by Davis, *Knightsbridge*, 54, and his followers.
12   Cf WAM, 4870; see Appendix (1478), 80.
13   Mapped in Gatty, *Mary Davies*, I, Plate 31. *Survey of London*, XLV, 19 and, following it, *VCH Middx*, XII, 135, suggest the Knightsbridge house.
14   *L&P Henry VIII*, vol. V, no. 627, 287–8; WAM, 16449, 7–11 Henry VIII.

from sources including parishioners of St Martin's: 'is and was imployed for the releife of the poore lame and impotent people of the saide hospitall'.[15] It was included in the subsequent hospital leases but was not in the pre-park ones.[16] The park itself would never have gone south of the main road but perhaps if the hospital site was trimmed this land was intended as compensation.

The 1460s were late for founding a leper hospital and as leprosy waned all such hospitals found more general uses.[17] Knightsbridge was one of six handed over to St Bartholomew's Hospital by the City in 1549, although neither the City nor Barts (with whom the link continued until 1623) ever had any ownership; the site and buildings, which included the lessee's residence, were always abbey property. It is unclear if the abbey ever cared about the lessees' medical competence. St Margaret's vestry provided a certificate of suitability for John Glassington during the Interregnum but probably only because he was holding precariously through a dean and chapter lease.[18] During the Interregnum the governors of the school and almshouses also sometimes nominated inmates but otherwise the abbey had no charitable involvement, and at least during the 16th and 17th centuries donations came from individuals and on occasion from the relevant parishes, which also sometimes nominated inmates and paid their costs.[19]

Glassington senior's 1595 report shows that the hospital was also serving as a place of indoor relief, a quasi-almshouse or workhouse.[20] The better off could also make arrangements for their old age: he agreed that Margaret Goulde could live out her days there, receiving food, drink and laundry facilities, provided she bequeathed the hospital her possessions.[21]

Davis, robustly sceptical of local myths, accepted the strong tradition that the hospital was used to isolate sufferers during the last great outbreak of plague in 1665–6, with those who died buried in a pit on Knightsbridge Green.[22] The John Glassington (re-)appointed in 1654 was a well-regarded surgeon but in 1668 the whole lazarcotes block was let to Nicholas Birkhead, probably a relation but certainly a goldsmith.[23] The hospital continued but had closed by 1718 when a new lease was granted to his widowed daughter-in-law.[24] 'Poore innocents' had been accommodated there in the 1630s and 1640s, and an orphanage or school for six boys and six girls continued until at least 1720, when she complained that reduced chapel collections had left her unable to clothe them. It had presumably closed before a charity school was established in a rear room in 1783. The complex survived as the White Hart inn and some ramshackle tenements until demolished in the early 1840s for Albert Gate.

15   WAM, 16453 m. 11.
16   WAM, 16298 (1473), 16293 (1527), 16289 (1619), 16306 (1654); *Survey of London*, XLV, 19 covers the site's later history.
17   For the unfootnoted parts of this section see *Religious Houses* and *Survey of London*, XLV, ch. 2.
18   WAM, 16316; *Religious Houses*, 323, has nothing for this John Glassington prior to 1654.
19   *Survey of London*, XLV, 41–2; Davis, *Knightsbridge*, 55–6.
20   WAM, 16311, cited by Lysons and thence by Davis, *Knightsbridge*, 54–5.
21   Merritt, *W (1)*, citing TNA, REC 2/213/21.
22   Davis, *Knightsbridge*, 145.
23   See *Survey of London*, XLV, ch. 2.
24   Cf 'Mrs Birkets Conduit' on Map 7 (1718), 50–1.

The Chapel

The chapel, mooted in 1473/4 and built by 1485, had the same private origin as the hospital, and as part of the Lazarcotes complex it too was in the parish of St Martin-in-the-Fields.[25] There is little information on its first century but by 1595 Glassington said that patients attended prayers there every morning and evening and were joined by neighbours on Sundays.[26] None can have been well served since this was not an official chapel of ease and there was no chaplain. The vicar of St Martin's sometimes came to administer communion, as in 1625 when he arrived by hired cart and also distributed provisions to the poor, but such visits cannot have been frequent.[27]

By 1629 the chapel was ruinous and the inhabitants of Knightsbridge petitioned the bishop of London for permission to rebuild. This was granted, with the consent of the vicar and churchwardens of St Martin's, but on condition that the congregation pay all the costs, that the chapel be consecrated to the use of the hospital, and that Knightsbridge's ordinary inhabitants attend their mother churches at least once a quarter and at Easter.[28] This new Trinity chapel, which was operating from the early 1630s, was always in a complicated position. It became for the first time an official chapel of ease of St Martin's but most of its population lived in St Margaret's, and the site continued to belong to the abbey's dean and chapter mediated through the lazarhouse lessees. In the late 17th and 18th centuries the lessees sub-let the chapel and the chapter appointed the sub-tenant as minister.[29]

The chapel's poverty was an ongoing problem and hopes that Trinity's pew rents would pay for the chaplain and repairs were soon disappointed. During the Interregnum the inhabitants petitioned Parliament for repair money from the proceeds of the sale of the dean and chapter lands, but presumably in vain.[30] The Knightsbridge lands had been sold to Sir George Stonehouse and c.1658–9 a list of ten donors to a fundraising campaign was headed by Lady Stonehouse, who gave 10s.[31] It was unfortunate that the Finches, owners of the grandest house in Knightsbridge from 1625/6 to 1689, treated Kensington as their local church. In 1699, when Knightsbridge's inhabitants again embarked on rebuilding and ran out of funds, they petitioned William III, newly installed as the Finches' successor, but the king was even less likely to relate to the chapel and the work is credited to Nicholas Birkhead, the lazarhouse lessee.[32]

The triple linkage with the abbey, St Martin's, and St Margaret's ensured that Knightsbridge reflected Westminster inhabitants' complex responses to the 17th century's

---

25   *VCH Middx*, XIII, 146–7 gives an account of the chapel that correctly assigns it to St Martin's, but within its section on St Margaret's. It also at 6–7 correctly describes the 1534 parish boundary changes; McMaster, *St Martin*, 332–3, followed by Honeybourne, 'Leper Hospitals', 41, asserted that these included the hospital's transfer to St Martin's.

26   WAM, 16311, cited by Lysons and thence by Davis, *Knightsbridge*, 54.

27   McMaster, *St Martin*, 332; Merritt, *W (1)*, 321, gives other examples from the 1610s and 1620s but perhaps underestimates Knightsbridge's pre-17th century-development.

28   Davis, *Knightsbridge*, 58–9; *Survey of London*, XLV, 41; *VCH Middx*, XIII, 146–7.

29   *VCH Middx*, XIII, 147.

30   *Survey of London*, XLV, 41.

31   Davis, *Knightsbridge*, 85–6, 15; later also published in J.H. Bloom (ed.), *Reg. of the Chapel of the Holy Trinity, Knightsbridge, 1658–1681* (n.d. c.1925). For Stonehouse's acquisition, WAM, 16323.

32   *VCH Middx*, XIII, 165.

Figure 20 *Knightsbridge chapel in 1767. See also the cover illustration, which shows the building after its 1789 alteration.*

upheavals.[33] It has long been known that Henry Walker (fl. 1638–60), ironmonger turned journalist and preacher, had become 'minister of God's word at Knightsbridge' by 1650 and that the inhabitants protested at Parliament's intrusion of 'a writer of weekly news'.[34] Two undated and carefully worded petitions to the governors of the school and almshouses add extra layers. In one the inhabitants stress their desire for 'a pious and zealous minister', protest against Walker and mention 'a very hopefull young man whom they pray may be settled there'.[35] In the other, 'out of desire to enjoy the gospel', they repeat their request for the removal of 'Mr Walker who hath intruded himself' and the reinstatement of 'Mr Wheatly one whom they very well approve and who hath also had his education in this school'. They understand that Walker has objected that Wheatly 'is a malignant and therefore not to be entertained amongst us for any minister' and request that if the objections are proved 'your petitioners may have the liberty of choosing some other godly man, which was never yet denied them'.[36] Only two possible Wheatl(e)ys are in the Westminster School lists. One, of whom nothing else, not even his first name, is known, was a pensioner in 1603; the other, Thomas, was 16 in 1648 and elected to Trinity

33   For the Westminster background, although not specifically the chapel, see Merritt, *W (1)* and *W (2)*.
34   Davis, *Knightsbridge*, 60–1, 64; *VCH Middx*, XIII, 147.
35   Hist. MSS Commission, *4th Rpt*, 188.
36   WAM, 9379.

College Cambridge in 1651.[37] The minister in 1660 was Thomas Wheatley but what had happened in the interim is unclear: Walker was allegedly on probation until 1655 when he was appointed curate, but he also certainly went on to other and richer ministries;[38] George Cooke is named as minister in 1653[39] and Christopher Lee in 1658.[40]

If Trinity had been a parish church its records would probably have survived better, although the absence of burial registers reflects the absence of a graveyard.[41] There are partial copies of baptismal registers between 1663 and 1702, although baptisms were occasionally performed up to the end of the 18th century.[42] The first reference to a marriage comes in 1632 from a bishop's register, and the chapel's own incomplete records run from 1658–1752.[43] Here the final date probably reflects Hardwick's Marriage Act (1753) which rendered invalid the marriages performed without banns that had been such chapels' specialism. Davis provided excellent examples of register entries marked 'secret' and of Knightsbridge featuring as an obvious place for clandestine marriages in *The Sullen Lover* (1668) and the *Guardian* (1713) but was unwilling to believe his own evidence, proposing that these were aberrations mostly limited to 1678–82.[44] He was unaware of the clerk at a bigamy trial at the Old Bailey in 1692 who produced a Knightsbridge register as evidence but conceded that 'it was usual for people to come there and to personate others, and to make sham marriages'.[45] The overall figures too are unmistakable, climbing way ahead of the population from 36 marriages in 1659 to 81 in 1661 and 335 in the second half of 1665; interestingly, though, they began to decline in the later 1670s: 424 in 1679, 394 in 1696, and in sharper stages thereafter, through 155 in 1698 and 45 in 1704 to 5 in 1747, 1 in 1751 and 2 in 1752.[46]

The decline was also wider. Davis lamented in 1859 that Knightsbridge was 'absurdly divided' between four parishes when its chapel 'could have been easily rendered the focus of a new and independent parish, had its patrons been so minded. The opportunity was lost when St George's was formed, and Trinity Chapel … was permitted to dwindle, without a thought for it, into comparative insignificance'.[47] St George's Hanover Square was formed in 1725, removing the whole of Eye from St Martin's. An increasing population had some impact on Trinity, which was enlarged to 300 seats in 1789.[48] By 1833, though, the incoming minister found it so dilapidated that congregations fell away in winter. He tried in vain to have it enlarged and its position regularised, noting bitterly in 1851 that the dean and chapter still treated Trinity as a proprietary chapel, let to the highest bidder and without proper funding or a regular district.

37   G.F. Russell Barker and A.H. Stenning (eds), *The Records of Old Westminsters*, 2 (1928), 984.

38   There is conflicting information in *ODNB*, s.a. Walker, Henry, journalist and preacher (accessed 6 Jan. 2016); Davis, *Knightsbridge*, 64; *VCH Middx*, XIII, 147.

39   *Cal. SP Dom.* 1652–3, 342.

40   Davis, *Knightsbridge*, 64.

41   Ibid., 66–7, laments the losses.

42   Ibid., 66, 70–3.

43   Ibid., 73–84.

44   Ibid., 67–9.

45   Bernard Capp, 'Bigamous marriage in early modern England', *Hist. Jnl*, 52 (2009), 553, citing Old Bailey t16920115-8.

46   Bloom, *Registers*, Davis, *Knightsbridge*, 90, n.

47   Davis, *Knightsbridge*, 51.

48   The remaining section is based on *VCH Middx*, XIII, 147 and *Survey of London*, XLV, 40–1.

The bad luck continued. An initial £2,000 promised by the Church Commissioners had not been spent when St Paul's Wilton Place opened in 1843, removing the immediate pressure, so the money was used for All Saints' Ennismore Gardens (1848–9, since 1955 a Russian Orthodox cathedral). As population growth continued, a rebuilding committee was formed in 1859 and the new 600-seat Holy Trinity chapel was opened on the same site in 1861 and assigned a district out of St Paul's and All Saints' in 1866. But Holy Trinity was demolished in 1904, despite considerable protest, when its replacement opened in Prince Consort Road, well away from the historic lazarhouse site and the hamlet.

It is appropriately occluding note on which to end. And more than a century after Kensington Palace was gifted to Kensington, there seems little point in campaigning for Knightsbridge Palace and Harrods of Kensington.

SOURCES AND ABBREVIATIONS

a.	acres
BL	British Library
Cal. Inq. p.m.	*Calendar of Inquisitions post-mortem*
Cal. Pat.	*Calendar of the Patent Rolls*
Cal. SP Dom.	*Calendar of State Papers, Domestic Series*
Chancellor, *Knightsbridge*	E. Beresford Chancellor, *Knightsbridge and Belgravia: Their History, Topography and Famous Inhabitants* (1909)
Conway Letters	M. Hope Nicolson (ed.), *The Conway Letters. The Correspondence of Anne, Viscountess Conway, Henry More and their Friends 1642–84* (1992)
Davis, 'Conduit System'	A. Morley Davis, 'London's First Conduit System: A Topographical Study', *Transactions of the London & Middlesex Archaeological Society*, n.s. 2 (1913), 9–59
Davis, *Knightsbridge*	H.G. Davis, *Memorials of the Hamlet of Knightsbridge* (1859)
Domesday	A. Williams and G.H. Martin (eds), *Domesday Book: A Complete Translation* (2002)
Faulkner, *Kensington*	T. Faulkner, *History and Antiquities of Kensington* (1820)
Fryman, *Kensington Palace*	O. Fryman (ed.), *Kensington Palace: Art, Architecture and Society* (forthcoming)
Gatty, *Mary Davies*	C.T. Gatty, *Mary Davies and the Manor of Ebury* (2 vols, 1921)
GDB	Great Domesday Book. Folio number followed by item number in *Domesday Book. Middlesex* (Phillimore edition, 1975)
Harvey, *WA Estates*	B. Harvey, *Westminster Abbey and its Estates in the Middle Ages* (1977)
Harvey, *Obedientiaries*	B. Harvey, *The Obedientiaries of Westminster Abbey and their Financial Records, c.1275–1540*, Westminster Abbey Records Series 3 (2002)
Hist. Parl. Commons 1604–29	A. Thrush and J.P. Ferris (eds), *The History of Parliament: the House of Commons 1604–1629*, (The History of Parliament Trust, 2010)

Hist. Parl. Commons *1660–90*	B.D Henning (ed.), *The History of Parliament: the House of Commons 1660–1690* (The History of Parliament Trust, 1983)
Impey, *Kensington Palace*	E. Impey, *Kensington Palace: The Official Illustrated History* (2003)
Keene, 'Knights'	D. Keene, '"Knights" before the Round Table: *Cnihtas*, Guildhalls and Governance in Early Winchester', in M. Henig and N. Ramsay (eds), *Intersections: The Archaeology and History of Christianity in England, 400–1200*, BAR British Series 505 (2010), 201–11
KCLS	Kensington & Chelsea Local Studies & Archives
L&P Henry VIII	Letters and Papers of Henry VIII
LGA 1899	*Local Government Act 1899. Enquiry as to the Westminster Boundaries* (available at KCLS)
LMA	London Metropolitan Archives
LUCHP	Land Use Consultants, 'Hyde Park' (1982). The current LUC Management Plan (2006, updated 2014), https://www.royalparks.org.uk/ has a far briefer historical summary.
LUCKG	Land Use Consultants, 'Kensington Gardens', cyclostyle (1982); copy at KCLS. The current LUC Management Plan (2007, updated 2014), https://www.royalparks.org.uk/ has a far briefer historical summary
McMaster, *St Martin*	J. McMaster, *A Short History of the Royal Parish of St Martin in the Fields* (1916)
Mason, *WA Charters*	E. Mason (ed.), *Westminster Abbey Charters*, London Record Society XXV (1988)
Merritt, *W (1)*	J.F. Merritt, *The Social World of Early Modern Westminster: Abbey, Court and Community 1525–1640* (2005)
Merritt, *W (2)*	J.F. Merritt, *Westminster 1640–60: A Royal City in a Time of Revolution* (2013)
ODNB	*Oxford Dictionary of National Biography* (www.oxforddnb.com)
Old OS Maps	*Old Ordnance Survey Maps*: edition published by Alan Godfrey, from 1983 (reduced facsimile reproduction of 1:2500 maps *c*.1865–1914). The relevant sheets are London 60 (1871, 1893, 1914), 61 (1870, 1894, 1914), 74 (1871, 1894, 1914), 75 (1869, 1894, 1916)
Pevsner, *Westminster*	S. Bradley and N. Pevsner, *London 6: Westminster* (2003)
PN Middx (EPNS)	*Place-Names of Middlesex*, (English Place-Name Society, vol. XVIII, 1942)
Religious Houses	C.M. Barron and M. Davies (eds), *The Religious Houses of London and Middlesex* (2007)
Rosser, *Medieval W*	G. Rosser, *Medieval Westminster 1200–1540* (1989)

Rutton, 'Eia'   W.L. Rutton, 'The Manor of Eia, or Eye next Westminster',
                                             Archaeologia, LXII (1910), 41–3, 142–5

Rutton, 'Hyde Park and   W.L. Rutton, 'Hyde Park and Kensington Gardens', *Notes &*
Kensington Gardens'   *Queries*, 10th ser., X (18 July and 22 Aug 1908)

Rutton, 'Kensington   W.L. Rutton, 'The Making of Kensington Gardens', *Home*
Gardens'   *Counties Magazine*, 6 (1904), 145–59, 222–31

S   Sawyer number, for Anglo-Saxon charters

Saunders, 'Extent of   G. Saunders, 'Results of an inquiry concerning the situation
Westminster'   and extent of Westminster, at various periods', *Archaeologia*,
                                             XXVI (1836), 223–41

Sullivan, *W Circle*   D. Sullivan, *The Westminster Circle* (2006)

Sullivan, *W Corridor*   D. Sullivan, *The Westminster Corridor* (1994)

Survey of London, XXXVII   *Survey of London*, vol. XXXVII, *Northern Kensington* (1973)

Survey of London, XXXVIII   *Survey of London*, vol. XXXVIII, *The Museums Area of South*
                                             Kensington and Westminster (1975)

Survey of London, XXXIX   *Survey of London*, vol. XXXIX, *The Grosvenor Estate in*
                                             Mayfair, Part 1 (General History) (1977)

Survey of London, XLI   *Survey of London*, vol. XLI, *Southern Kensington: Brompton*
                                             (1983)

Survey of London, XLV   *Survey of London*, vol. XLV, *Knightsbridge* (2000)

TNA   The National Archives

Valor Eccl.   *Valor Ecclesiasticus, temp. Hen VIII* (Record Commission,
                                             1810–34)

VCH   *Victoria County History*

WAM   Westminster Abbey Muniments

WCA   Westminster City Archives

Three Descriptions of Lands Later Included in Hyde Park and Kensington Gardens

A   The demesnes between the two main roads farmed with Hyde in 1478[1]

Scribes always found place-names difficult, and perhaps because this is a draft document the spellings are exceptionally inconsistent. This summary indicates the range but there are a few insurmountable difficulties. The scribe frequently deployed his 'e' form for both 'e' and 'a' and, when he wrote a distinct 'a', used it interchangeably with 'e' in words such as 'Way'. He was also inconsistent on upper and lower case and on spacing. Most such variants are unimportant so uncertainties are not indicated below, and the first word in each name has been standardised to upper case. More problematically, the scribe used a sign after a terminal 't' with enough consistency to suggest the standard contraction for '–es' (or '–is', as in boscis) rather than a simple flourish. On the other hand the resultant examples of –shottes contrast both with the same shot names in other documents and with this document's use elsewhere of –shote. These questionable extensions are indicated below as (es).

The items and their abuttals are given in the order in which they appear. Where an abuttal does not have its own entry any additional description is given in brackets.

> Site of Hide manor with all the buildings (unspecified) inside the moat; outside the moat a grange, stable, Cowehous, Shapehous, Heyhous also called Coppydhall, a house at the Gate called Deyhous (ie dairy) with two rooms above it, another house called Gateloft and a dovecot

> Fields:
> **Name**, Description, Abuttals

> **Kensyngton medow**
> pasture close
> Cranysfeld w and n, Otefeld e, Wyndesorewey s

1   WAM, 4870. I am grateful to Matthew Payne for discussion. The descriptive detail was shorn from the final version, WAM, Reg. Bk I, ff. 20–20v.

Otefeld

pasture field

Cranysfeld and Dawberisshote (pasture close held by copy of court roll) w, Brokeshote
   alias Kyngesdowne e, Kensyngton medow and aforesaid road s, Tadycroft and
   Fyrsyfeld n

Tadycroft magna

pasture close

Halfhide (croft held by copy of court roll) and Lytyltadycroft (pasture croft held by
   bishop of Bath) w, Rowelond (w, but mistake for) e, Otefeld s, Acton Wey n

Rowelond

pasture close

Otefeld s, Acton Wey n, Tadycroft magna w, Fyrsefeld e

Fyrsefeld

Rowelond w, rivulet from Bayardeswatering e to Brokeshote, Otefeld and Brokeshote
   s, Acton Wey n

Gret Bromehyll

pasture close

rivulet from Bayardeswatering w, Puggescroft (pasture croft), new ditch planted with
   vines and la Hidegrove e, Brokeshote s, Acton Wey n

Longmedow

7 acres of meadow within Gret Bromehill

lying along the rivulet from Beyardeswateryng to le Shepynbrigge

Lityll Bromehyll

arable croft taken from Gret Bromehyll

Gret Bromehyll w, Conyngar e, le Hydegrove s, Puggescroft n

Lytylconyngger

arable close now separated from Greteconyngger

Bromehyll w, Shepeleys e, Greteconyngger s, Galowmede n

Galowmede

meadow

Litilconyngger s, Acton Wey n, Litill Bromehyll w, Galowfeld e

Galowfeld

arable croft

Galowmede w, Mablescroft (arable croft of abbot and convent) e, Lytylconyngar and
   Shepeleys s, Acton Wey n

Hidegrove

grove

Hidecroft alias Homecroft (croft next to site of manor) s, Lytyll Bromehyll n, Grete
   Bromehyll w, Gretconyngger e

Gretconyngger

pasture close now separated from another pasture (sic) close called Lytylconyggar

Shepehousgarden (garden) and site of manor close s, Lytylconyggar n, Hydegrove w,
   Shepeleys e

Shepeleys

pasture close

Cresswelshott(es) alias Homefeld s and e, Galowfeld n, Gret and Lityl Conyyngar w

Motecroft
pasture close
Bromehill w, moat of site of manor e, aforesaid rivulet s, Hidegrove n
Barnecroft(es)
pasture croft
Motecroft w, road from Shepynbrygge e, aforesaid rivulet s, site of manor n
Hoggescroft
Barnecroft(es) w, road from Shepynbrygge e, aforesaid rivulet s, le Shepehous n
Garden outside site of manor moat
moat w, Hoggcroft e, Barnecroft(es) s, large grange called Hidebarne n
Kyngesdowne alias Hillond
meadow or pasture close lately arable
Otefeld w, 1 acre pasture e (lately arable, pertaining to heirs of Robert Orchard,
    separated by a boundary mark), Wyndesor Wey s, footpath called Warrenlwey n
25 acres meadow or pasture lately arable in Brokeshot
Otefeld w, land of Nicholas Norton e, Warrenlwey s, aforesaid rivulet n
Welplotte
pasture close
Wyndesorewey s, 3 acres in Brokeshot (pasture pertaining to heirs of Richard Hoo)
    and Horselees n, Hillond alias Kyngesdowne w, pasture close (site of manor of
    Knightsbridge, at farm to Robert Orchard) e
Horseleys
pasture close
aforesaid 3 acres in Brokeshote w, le Hooke e, Welplotte and site of said manor s,
    aforesaid rivulet n
Le Hooke
meadow
Horseleys, site of said manor and pasture close of Robert Orchard next to
    Brownespond w, Cressewell e, pasture close of Robert Orchard, pasture close of
    Robert Noreys and orchard and grove of heirs of Richard Hoo s, aforesaid rivulet n
Cressewall
croft (said above to be meadow or pasture)
Le Hooke and Cresswalshott(es) alias Homefeld w, Stonehill e, Wyndesor Wey s,
    Cresswalshott(es) n
Cresswelshott(es) alias Homefeld
pasture close
site of manor of Hide and Shepeleys w, Stonehyll (pasture) and road to
    Hodilston(es)pitt(es)[2] e, aforesaid rivulet and meadow called Cressewell s,
    Galowcroft(es) and Mabelcroft n

2   There is an upward line from the 'n' that probably indicates a contraction, as well as the regular sign on
    the terminal 't'.

Exclusions:
all regalities, woods, subwoods, acre borders and hedgerows
a bank or parcel of land at Knightsbridge, 3 foot wide on n for ditch-scouring and
    carriage and for repair to lez lazarcotes
a road built for the passage of the abbey's tenants of Knightsbridge and Westbourne
    and for bringing waifs and strays into the demesne, from the s entry on Wyndesor
    Wey called Oldeweygate to the n exit onto Acton Wey by Northweygate

B   Two Rich – Coppin sales, 9 July 1616[3] and 12 July 1619[4]

Description, Additional Information, Parish, Abuttals
Parishes: St M: St Margaret's; P: Paddington: Ken: Kensington

9 July 1616

**3 parcels of pasture: Long Parke Close, part of an unnamed meadow, part of the
    Brome close, now forming a single 11½ acre close**
St M
Hyde Park e, pasture of Agmundesham Muschampe called Crane Feild s and Riche's
    land s, w and n

2 July 1619

**Messuage or tenement called the White Hart and nearby tenement or house and
    extensive appurtenances**
White Hart let to Robert Prudam, previously to John Wescott decd; other previously
    let to John Stoning gent decd
St M
1 acre meadow or pasture
 part of said premises s
3½ acres meadow and pasture
lately severed from close called the Moore
said acre s
5 acres arable, pasture or meadow
lately part of the Bromefeild, otherwise called parcel of the nine acres, now joined
    with the 3½ acres
said 3½ acres s
4 acres meadow or pasture
St M and Ken or one of them
Park Close s, Hyde Park e
4 acres land or pasture
P, Ken, St M or some or one of them
London to Acton highway n, Hyde Park e

3   TNA, C 54 230/7.
4   TNA, C 54 2417/11.

9 acres pasture called the half hyde
now divided into 2 parcels
St M and P
said highway n, the nyne acres and Thomas his feild w
The nyne acres, pasture
P and St M
Ken vicarage land w, Thomas his feild n
The Pondd Close, 1 acre 1 rod pasture
Cranefeild e, White Hart s
Messuage lately divided into two, and extensive appurtenances
let to Francis Raunce and John Blagrave, previously to Richard Spirwicke of Ken, cook
    decd
Ken, St M, P or some or one of them
Thomas his feild, 7 acre close or field of land or pasture
Ken, St M, P or some or one of them
London to Acton highway n, gravel pits now in occupation of Francis Raunce and
    previously of Richard Spirwicke w

With all other Rich lands etc pertaining to any of said messuages lying in said parishes
    between London to Acton highway n, London to Brentford highways, Hyde Park
    pale, land lately purchased by Coppin and Crane Field e, gravel pits, vicarage land,
    Cunduite Close and land late William Muschampe w

INDEX

CPSIA information can be obtained
at www.ICGtesting.com
Printed in the USA
JSHW022225211219
3115JS00002B/17